Contents

Teacher Tips

Encourage Topic Interest

Help students develop an understanding and appreciation of different STEM concepts by providing an area in the classroom to display topic-related non-fiction books, pictures, collections, and artifacts as a springboard for learning.

What I Think I Know / What I Would Like to Know Activity

Introduce each STEM unit by asking students what they think they know about the topic, and what they would like to know about the topic. Complete this activity as a whole-group brainstorming session, in cooperative small groups, or independently. Once students have had a chance to complete the questions, combine the information to create a class chart for display. Throughout the study, periodically update students' progress in accomplishing their goal of what they want to know, and validate what they think they know.

Vocabulary List

Keep track of new and theme-related vocabulary on chart paper for students' reference. Encourage students to add theme-related words. Classify the word list into the categories of nouns, verbs, and adjectives. In addition, have students create their own STEM dictionaries as part of their learning logs.

Learning Logs

Keeping a learning log is an effective way for students to organize thoughts and ideas about the STEM concepts presented and examined. Students' learning logs also provide insight on what follow-up activities are needed to review and to clarify concepts learned.

Learning logs can include the following types of entries:

- Teacher prompts
- Students' personal reflections
- Questions that arise
- Connections discovered
- Labelled diagrams and pictures
- Definitions for new vocabulary

Your Respiratory System

In and out, in and out. You do not even think about it, but you breathe constantly. You have to, since breathing brings in the oxygen your cells need to work. Breathing also takes away the carbon dioxide that the cells produce.

The Respiratory Route

When you breathe in, air enters your nose and mouth and flows into your nasal cavity. There, it is warmed and cleaned. Air then flows down the main part of your throat, or pharynx, to your larynx which contains your vocal cords. Then air enters the trachea, or windpipe, which branches into two bronchial tubes—one leading to each lung. Those tubes branch into many smaller tubes called bronchioles. Your lungs are at the end of this system of tubes.

Oxygen In, Carbon Dioxide Out

At the end of the bronchioles are bundles of air sacs called alveoli. There, your blood picks up the oxygen you breathe in and drops off the carbon dioxide you breathe out.

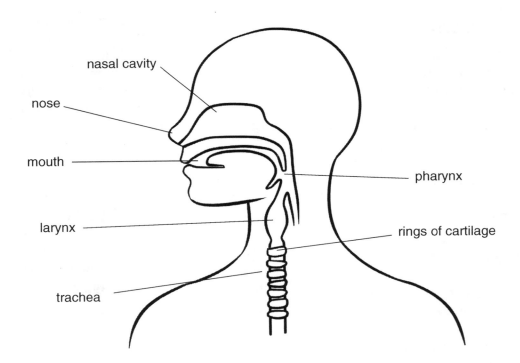

continued next page ☞

Lung Action

You have two lungs: right and left.

Under the lungs is a muscle called the diaphragm. When this muscle pulls down, your lungs expand and fill with air. You breathe in. When the diaphragm relaxes, air is pushed out of the lungs. You breath out. When you are just sitting, you breathe about 20 times each minute. That number can double when you are running.

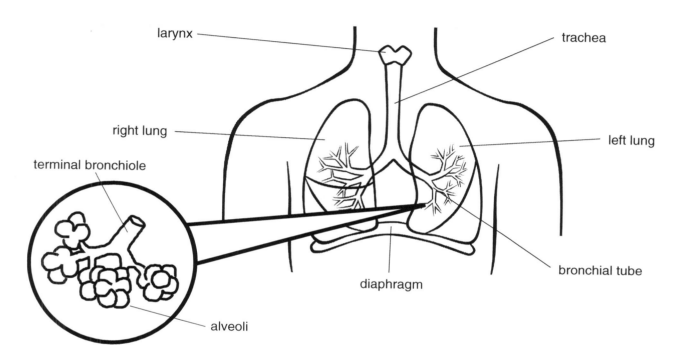

larynx

trachea

right lung

left lung

terminal bronchiole

bronchial tube

diaphragm

alveoli

Sticky and Slimy

In your nose, mucous glands produce a slimy substance called mucus. Mucus keeps your nose moist, and traps dirt and germs. It helps keep you healthy.

Feel Those Rings

Your trachea is made of rings of firm, flexible cartilage. You can run your fingertips up and down the front of your neck to feel these rings.

Up in Smoke

Healthy lungs are pink and clean. But the lungs of a smoker are dark grey and full of dirt. That is because chemicals in cigarette smoke damage the trachea. It can no longer keep the dirt out. Also, the smallest tubes in the lungs fill up with tar from the cigarettes. Because of this, a smoker's lungs do not work well and make breathing difficult.

1. The diagram below shows the route air takes when we breathe. (White arrows show inhaling, and dark arrows show exhaling.) Complete the diagram by naming parts of the respiratory system.

a) The two places where we inhale and exhale: _____ and _____

b) The space in the nose where air is warmed and cleaned: _____

c) The main part of the throat: _____

d) The tube in the throat that contains the vocal cords: _____

e) What directs air into the right or left lung: _____

f) Small air passages at the ends of the bronchial tubes: _____

g) Where oxygen is added to blood and carbon dioxide is removed: _____

2. List ways your respiratory system can be affected when you have a cold.

_____

_____

_____

_____

_____

Experiment: How Much Air?

How much air is in a single breath you take? Try this experiment to find out.

What You Need

- Sink or large bowl
- Water
- Bendable straw
- 2-L plastic pop bottle with cap
- Measuring cup
- Partner

What You Do

1. Completely fill the pop bottle with water and screw on the cap. Then fill the sink or bowl with water until it is about half full.

2. Turn the bottle upside down and hold it in the water so the cap is underwater. Remove the cap while it is underwater. Make sure no air gets inside the bottle.

3. Have your partner hold the bottle for you. Place one end of the straw in the opening of the bottle. Take a deep breath and blow into the straw. The air you blow out will go into the bottle.

4. While your partner holds the top of the bottle underwater, screw the cap back on.

5. Lift the bottle out of the water. Turn it upright and remove the cap. Fill the measuring cup with water. (Do not use the water from the bottle.) Record how much water is in the measuring cup.

6. Slowly pour water from the measuring cup into the bottle until it is full. Look at the markings on the measuring cup. Check how much water it took to fill the bottle.

7. Repeat the experiment, letting your partner blow air into the bottle this time.

Think About It!

1. How much water did it take to refill the bottle?

   You: _____ Your partner: _____

2. What was the amount (volume) of water you poured into the bottle in step 6? What volume of air did you breathe into the bottle in step 3? Explain why the volumes are the same.

   _____

   _____

   _____

Your Circulatory System

The circulatory system delivers food and oxygen to your body's cells. These fuels are carried in your blood. Blood takes waste to your kidneys. It also transports messenger chemicals throughout your body.

Have a Heart

Your heart is a muscle about the size of your fist. Blood enters the heart, then gets pumped to the lungs to pick up oxygen. Blood also drops off carbon dioxide in your lungs. This blood then goes back through the heart, where it is pumped throughout your body.

In just one day, your heart beats about 100 000 times. It pumps 7600 L of blood every day. The heart is a very hard-working muscle.

Blood Vessels

Blood vessels are tubes that transport your blood. Arteries carry oxygen-rich blood away from the heart to the cells of your body. Your veins carry the oxygen-poor blood from those cells back to the heart.

This network would be about 100 000 km long, stretched out.

That Amazing Red Stuff

The body of an average adult contains 5 L of blood. Each droplet carries food, chemicals, waste, and billions of blood cells throughout your body.

In each drop of blood:

    375 000 white blood cells fight germs and infections
  13 000 000 platelets help your blood form scabs
250 000 000 red blood cells carry the oxygen cells need

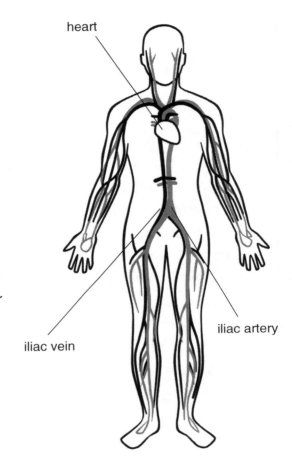

heart

iliac vein

iliac artery

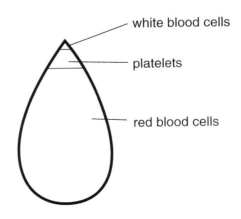

white blood cells

platelets

red blood cells

1. Count Your Pulse Rate

Each time your heart beats, blood flows through your arteries. The arteries swell slightly as blood flows through them. This temporary swelling is called a pulse. You can feel it in places where your arteries are close to your skin. Two places to feel your pulse are your wrist and neck.

Find out what your pulse rate is. Place a finger on the inside of your wrist. Do not use your thumb. Can you feel a beat? Count your pulse for one minute.

a) My resting pulse is _____ beats per minute.

Jog on the spot or run outside for a few minutes. Then take your pulse.

b) My active pulse is _____ beats per minute.

c) Which number is higher? _____

2. Multiple Pulses

Place two fingers of your right hand on the right side of your neck. Place them just below your jaw. You will feel a pulse as your carotid artery carries blood to your head.

Keep your fingers on your neck. Place the fingers of your left hand on your right wrist to feel the pulse there.

a) Focus on the two pulses you can feel. Which pulse is stronger?

_____

b) Which pulse can you feel first?

_____

c) How can you explain these results?

_____

_____

_____

_____

Your Digestive System

Oxygen is an important fuel for your body, and so is food. Food gives your body's cells energy to breathe, move, and do many other things. Food also provides your body with proteins, vitamins, and minerals.

Take a Bite

Digestion starts when you take a bite of food. The food is ground up and wetted. Then your tongue pushes it back to your esophagus which squeezes it down to your stomach.

Down in the Stomach

Your stomach is a big bag where the food gets broken down. The muscles in your stomach squeeze the food. Digestive juices dissolve the food. These juices are made in your liver, pancreas, and gall bladder.

Your Two Intestines

From your stomach, the food moves into a crooked tube called the small intestine. This is where the nutrients are extracted from the food. Anything left over moves down into the large intestine or colon. There, water is soaked up and the waste is formed into lumps.

Taking Out the Garbage

The leftover waste then moves into your excretory system. Extra water, or urine, goes into the bladder. It is stored there until you go to the bathroom. Solid waste leaves your body through a tube called the rectum.

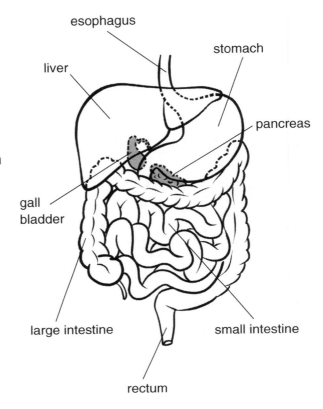

esophagus

stomach

liver

pancreas

gall bladder

large intestine

small intestine

rectum

"Your Digestive System"—Think About It!

1. List, from first to last, the organs food passes through in your digestive system.

small intestine   rectum   stomach   esophagus   large intestine   mouth

a) _____   d) _____

b) _____   e) _____

c) _____   f) _____

2. Which of the organs listed in question 1 are tubes? Circle them in the list.

3. How could you make a model of the digestive system? Write a list of materials you could use. Match each material to a part of the digestive system. If there is time, work with a group to build the model.

_____

_____

_____

_____

_____

_____

_____

4. Touch a Tooth: Your teeth are an important part of your digestive system. Wash your hands carefully. Then feel the shapes of your teeth.

a) Which teeth would be good for biting pieces off an apple? Why do you think so?

_____

_____

b) Which teeth would be good for crushing food? Explain.

_____

_____

_____

Your Bones and Skeleton

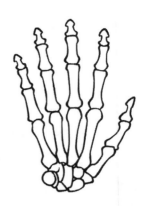

Adults have 206 bones. Each hand has 27 bones and each foot has 26.

Bones have many shapes. Your 12 pairs of ribs are curved. They form a protective cage around your chest. There is a straight bone running down each leg from the hip to the knee. This thigh bone is the longest bone in your body. Your body's smallest bone is in the ear. It is shaped like a stirrup on a horse's saddle.

Down at the Corner

Bones connect to other bones at joints. You have about 360 joints, including your knees, elbows, and hips. Cartilage is a tough, flexible tissue. It covers the ends of bones in joints. Cartilage also shapes your nose and ears.

Joints are held together by ligaments. Ligaments are straps of strong, flexible tissue. There are different types of joints in your body because they have different jobs to do. They also have to move in different ways. For example, your knee is a hinge joint. It moves like a hinge on a door.

Think About It!

1. Look at the types of joints shown below. Move your body. Can you find joints on your body that might look like these? Write your ideas.

   a) Hinge joint _____

   b) Ball-and-socket joint _____

   c) Pivot joint  _____

2. Give an example of how bones support your body.

   _____

3. How do bones protect your body? Give an example.

   _____

4. How do bones and joints help you move? Explain.

   _____
   _____

The Muscles of Your Body

Your bones and joints need muscles to help them move. There are about 660 muscles in your body. Skeletal muscles shape the body and hold it upright.

Another important muscle is your diaphragm. It is a dome-shaped muscle below your lungs. This muscle squeezes your lungs when you breathe out. Muscles in your intestines work without you thinking about them.

Pulling in Pairs

Muscles can only pull bones and joints, they cannot push them. So muscles often work in pairs. For example, the biceps muscle bends your arm. Your triceps muscle straightens your arm. It does this by pulling on the back of your elbow. Touch your arm and you will feel them working.

Tough Tendons

Each muscle narrows into a cord at the end. This is dense, tough tissue known as a tendon. Tendons are attached to bones. When the muscle contracts, the tendon pulls on the bone.

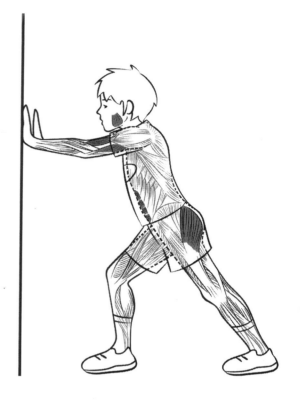

The jaw muscle is the strongest muscle in your body. Your tongue is a muscle that helps you communicate and eat. It takes about 16 muscles to smile.

"The Muscles of Your Body"—Think About It!

1. a) List at least four occupations in which having strong muscles is important. Justify your thinking.

_____

_____

_____

b) List three ways muscles are used by people who work at a desk all day. Justify your thinking.

_____

_____

_____

2. Which muscle helps you breathe? _____

_____

_____

3. Which muscles bend your arms? _____

_____

_____

4. Which muscles straighten your arms? _____

_____

_____

5. Which muscle pumps your blood? _____

_____

_____

Touch a Tendon

You can feel your Achilles tendon. It is one of the largest tendons in your body. Pinch your lower leg, just above your heel. The tendon feels hard like a bone. But when you press it, it bends slightly. The Achilles tendon joins the muscles in your calf to your heel. This is so you can pull up your foot when you walk.

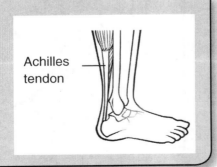

Achilles tendon

Your Nervous System

Feeling, seeing, hearing, moving, thinking. You can do all of these things at the same time, thanks to your nervous system. It is the control centre of your body. It automatically regulates many of your body's processes.

The Brains Behind the Operation

The central nervous system is made up of your brain and spinal cord. They are linked to your body through a network of nerve cells.

Nerves use electricity and chemicals to transmit messages. These messages go to and from your brain.

Making Sense

You have five senses: sight, hearing, smell, taste, and touch. Your eyes, ears, nose, mouth, and skin all send messages to your brain. The brain processes the messages and allows you to sense and react to your environment.

A Matter of Survival

Your nervous system is important for your survival. For example, if you touch something hot, you quickly move your hand away. That reaction is automatic—a reflex. If you see a car racing toward you, your eyes send a message to your brain. Your brain delivers a message to your feet to start running.

Your five senses communicate with your brain while you eat a snow cone.

cold   crunchy
sweet   grape
purple

continued next page

Your Amazing Nervous System

There are thousands of kilometres of nerves in your body. Laid out end to end, your nerves would wrap around Earth twice! Nerves carry messages at the speed of 430 km/h.

There are neurons that run from your spinal cord to your toes. They are the longest cells in your body. They are incredibly narrow, but are up to 1.2 m long.

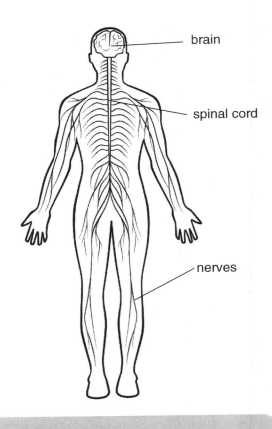

brain

spinal cord

nerves

Think About It!

1. Write a description about the work your nerves did during a game you played. Use the information you read and your own ideas. (**Hint:** Remember your body as well as your senses.)

_____

_____

_____

_____

Feed Your Brain

You sleep and do not eat during the night. Your brain needs fuel when you wake up. Experts have shown that "hungry" brains have trouble remembering things. They also have trouble learning new information. So do your brain a favour—eat breakfast! Protein foods are very good "brain foods" for breakfast. Protein foods include eggs and nuts. Oatmeal cereal and whole-grain bread are also good breakfast foods.

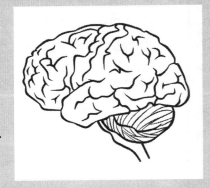

Experiment 1: Test Your Reflexes

Here is a simple experiment to test your reflexes. You will need a ruler and a partner.

1. Hold the ruler near the end with the highest number and let the ruler hang down. Have your partner put his or her hand at the bottom of the ruler. Your partner should get ready to grab the ruler. But they should not be touching the ruler.

2. Tell your partner that you will drop the ruler soon. Your partner should grab the ruler as soon as possible after you drop it. Record the level in centimetres where he or she catches the ruler. Try the experiment a few times, changing how soon you drop the ruler. Then switch roles and try it again.

The smaller the number of centimetres, the faster your reflexes. What happens when you repeat the experiment a number of times? Can you catch the ruler more quickly? Try the experiment in dim light. Record your results. Are your reflexes faster or slower?

Experiment 2: Find Your Blind Spot

You may think your vision is pretty good, but did you know you have a blind spot? That is a place where you cannot see anything. Normally you do not notice your blind spot. Here is an experiment to help you find it.

1. Close your right eye and hold this page at arm's length.
2. Look at the dot with your left eye. You should also be able to see the plus sign.
3. Move the page slowly toward you. The plus sign will disappear at a certain point.

You can test your right eye by closing your left eye. Then focus on the plus sign.

What is happening? Blood vessels and a major nerve pass through a place at the back of your eyeball. Millions of cells in your eyes receive images and send information to your brain. But there are no cells at that particular place, so you have a blind spot.

Experiment 3: Trick Your Brain

Cross the index and middle finger of one hand. Now touch your nose with your crossed fingertips. For most people, it feels as though they have two noses. Why do you think this is?

_____

_____

_____

_____

Overview of the Human _____ System

Write a description of this system.

List the parts of the body that make up this system.

How do these parts work together?

How does the body use this system?

Sunlight and Vitamin D

You have to make decisions about how to keep your body fit. You decide what to eat and how to get enough exercise. You may also decide to stay out of the sunlight and not allow your skin to burn.

Skin cancer caused by being out in the sunlight too much is a health concern. But people need sunlight to make vitamin D. How can you get enough of this nutrient without damaging your skin?

Why You Need Vitamin D

Vitamin D helps bones grow and stay strong. Calcium and other minerals are stored in bones. Your bones need vitamin D to absorb these minerals properly.

Why Do People Not Get Enough Vitamin D?

Your body makes a lot of vitamin D when it gets sunlight. People may avoid sunlight to protect their skin. Where you live can also make it difficult to get vitamin D from sunlight. Why? You may have to cover up to be warm or to cool off. Also, sunlight gets weaker as you move away from the equator. So people who live far from the equator do not get enough vitamin D.

Sunscreen also reduces the amount of sunlight your skin receives. Sunscreen with an SPF of 15 can block 99 percent of your body's vitamin D production.

Brain Stretch

On a separate piece of paper, draft a persuasive radio commercial to promote the benefits of vitamin D. Share it with your class. Use this checklist to help you:

❏ My commercial is 15 to 30 seconds long.

❏ My commercial has a clear message about the benefits of vitamin D.

❏ I created the commercial to appeal to my target audience. (kids or adults)

❏ I practiced reading my commercial with expression.

"Sunlight and Vitamin D"—Think About It!

1. What are some things you can do to avoid sun damage to your skin?

_____

_____

_____

2. You need one hour of sunlight each week. Fill in the chart below. Show how many minutes of sunlight you get (on average) each day.

	Mon.	Tues.	Wed.	Thurs.	Fri.	Sat.	Sun.
Amount of sunlight in minutes							

Total amount of sunlight in an average week: _____ minutes.

If you did not get one hour of sunlight in a week, what could you do to get more?

_____

_____

3. List some advantages and disadvantages of spending more time outside in the sunlight.

Advantages	Disadvantages

Healthy Eating: Journal Topics

Eating a balanced diet is an important way of taking care of your body. Here are some questions to get you thinking about your eating habits.

1 Why do you think it is important to eat a balanced diet?

2 How do you think what you eat affects your body and the way you feel?

3 Do you think the media influences your eating habits? Explain your thinking.

4 What do you think the differences are between a snack and a treat?

5 Do your eating habits change? Do you eat differently when you are at home than when you are with your friends or out at a restaurant? Explain.

6 What can you do to maintain a healthy body weight?

7 Do you like to eat breakfast? Why or why not?

8 Are there any foods you refuse to eat? Explain.

9 Name some of your favourite foods. Why are they your favourite?

10 Do you check the nutritional information on the food items you eat? Why or why not?

11 Do you think convenience foods (frozen foods, canned foods, fast food) make it easier or more difficult to keep a healthy diet? Explain your thinking.

Fitness and Health

Your body is made of systems. These include your respiratory system and muscular system. They work together to help you do all the things you want to do. It is important to keep each of these systems healthy by staying fit. You can do this through regular exercise.

It Is Great to Be Fit!

When you are fit, your heart can pump more efficiently. Your muscles are also stronger. You are more flexible and your joints move more easily. You do not get sick as often and your injuries heal faster. You also have improved balance. This makes you better at sports such as skiing, kayaking, and hockey.

Feel Good

Are you feeling stressed? Staying fit can help. People who exercise feel less stress. And exercising actually puts you in a better mood. When you work out, your brain releases chemicals that make you feel happier.

Zzzzzz

People who are fit sleep better. They fall asleep faster and they sleep more soundly.

Smoking

An easy way to help stay fit and healthy is to not smoke. Smoking damages your respiratory system. It also affects your whole body, since all of your systems are linked.

Every Day

You need about 60 minutes of exercise every day. That sounds like a lot, but you get exercise every time you walk up the stairs or walk to a friend's home. You also get exercise when you pick up a stack of books. Try to work all of your muscles every day by doing a variety of exercises.

Staying fit all your life will help you live longer and healthier.

"Fitness and Health"—Think About It!

1. List at least four ways to stay healthy.

_____

_____

_____

_____

2. Complete the web below on the benefits of staying fit.

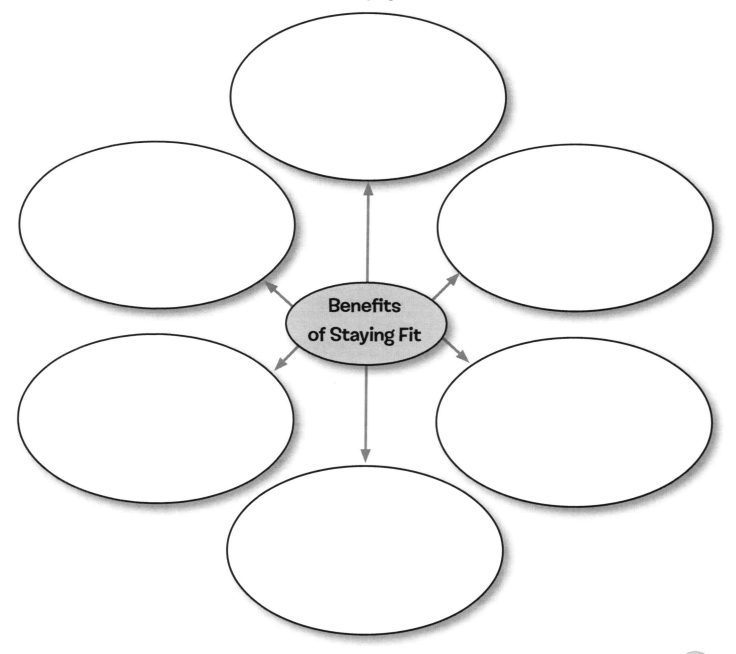

Create a Human Body Board Game

What You Do

1. Choose a base for the game board.
2. Create a path the game pieces will follow. You may choose to give your path a specific shape: a U shape, an L shape, a square, or an oval. Make your path at least 50 squares long.
3. Add spaces where you have to stack question cards cut from heavy paper. Print or handwrite questions on the cards. Print instructions on some game board spaces.
4. Test the game to see if it is too hard or has enough spaces.
5. Cut small figures out of paper to use as game pieces, or use materials that are available.
6. Decorate the game board to make it colourful so people know it is about the human body.
7. Write the rules and directions on how to play the game.

Rules and How to Play

- How does a player move around the board? Here are some ideas:
  - roll the number cubes
  - pick up a card and answer a question
  - follow the instructions on the game board spaces
- Are there penalties for wrong answers?
- How many people can play?

Ideas for Game Cards

Create questions about the human body to test players' knowledge. Create different categories such as

- true or false
- explain
- multiple choice

Ideas for Game Board Spaces

- miss a turn
- go back 5 spaces
- roll again

Two Basic Forces: Pushing and Pulling

A force is something that can make an object change speed, shape, or direction. The forces of push and pull can do all three of these things. Here are some examples.

Pushing

- You are coasting along on a skateboard and you want to go faster. You use your foot to push backward on the sidewalk. This push gives you more speed.
- You have a wet ball of clay. You push down on it. The force of pushing changes the shape of the clay. It is no longer in the shape of a ball.
- A soccer ball is rolling toward you. You can push it in another direction.

Pulling

- You let go of a shopping cart on a hill, and it rolls away from you. You catch up with the cart and pull on it. By pulling, you change the speed of the shopping cart.
- You pull at each end of an elastic band to make the elastic change its shape.
- You play with a yo-yo. You let go of the yo-yo to make it drop toward the ground. When the yo-yo reaches the end of the string, you give it a quick upward pull. The yo-yo then changes direction and travels up, instead of down.

The Pulling Force of Gravity

Gravity is a force that pulls objects down toward Earth. When you let go of a ball, gravity is what makes the ball drop to Earth. Now, think about what happens when you throw a ball up in the air. Gravity slows down the speed of the ball until it stops travelling upward. Then gravity makes the ball start to travel down to the ground. The closer the ball gets to the ground, the faster it moves. This shows how the pulling force of gravity changes the speed and the direction of the ball.

Brain Stretch

What pushes and pulls can you see around you? How did you use forces today? Describe them on a separate piece of paper.

"Two Basic Forces: Pushing and Pulling"—Think About It!

1. Describe how you use the forces of pushing and pulling when you do the following activities.

   a) Use a computer mouse: _____

   _____

   _____

   b) Brush your teeth: _____

   _____

   _____

   c) Ride a bicycle: _____

   _____

   _____

2. Choose a sport (other than cycling) that you enjoy playing or watching. Explain how the forces of pushing and/or pulling are involved in playing the sport. If gravity plays a role, explain what it does.

   _____

   _____

   _____

   _____

   _____

   _____

3. When you blow up a balloon, your lungs push air into the balloon. Which does this pushing force cause a change in: speed, shape, or direction? Explain your answer.

   _____

   _____

   _____

   _____

   _____

   _____

Forces and Structures

What Is a Structure?

A structure is something that holds or supports a load. For example, a garden shed has four walls that support a roof.

Structures are built for one or more purposes. A garden shed provides a place to keep garden tools dry. A locked shed will also keep the tools safe so they will not be stolen.

What Types of Forces Act on Structures?

Two types of forces act on structures—internal forces and external forces.

Internal forces are part of the structure. For example, the roof of a house is heavy and pushes down on the outside walls. The roof is part of the structure of the house. If the walls are not strong enough to hold up the roof, the house will collapse. So the pushing force created by the weight of the roof is an internal force.

External forces come from things that are not part of the structure. For example, snow will push its weight down on the roof. The walls also have to be strong enough to support the weight of snow on the roof. Because the snow is not part of the structure, snow is an external force.

Two Types of Loads

Loads are forces that act on a structure. All structures need to be strong enough to hold up under the loads placed on them. Loads are divided into two categories—dead loads and live loads.

A **dead load** is a permanent load that does not leave. The weight of the materials used to build a structure are part of the dead load. Anything permanently attached to a structure is part of the dead load. Carpet and window planters are dead loads.

A **live load** is a load that is temporary. Objects that carry temporary loads are also part of the live load. Here are some examples:

- Furniture is part of the live load in a house. Furniture can be removed from the house if you move to a new house.
- Snow that builds up on a house roof is a live load. Snow is temporary because it can melt away or be removed.

1. For each example below, identify whether it is a live load or a dead load. Explain your thinking.

a) Plumbing pipes

☐ live load   ☐ dead load

Why I think so: _____

_____

_____

b) An elevator in an office building

☐ live load   ☐ dead load

Why I think so: _____

_____

_____

c) The people who work in an office building

☐ live load   ☐ dead load

Why I think so: _____

_____

_____

d) Wind that blows against a structure on windy days

☐ live load   ☐ dead load

Why I think so: _____

_____

_____

e) The balconies in an apartment building

☐ live load   ☐ dead load

Why I think so: _____

_____

_____

Four Types of Internal Forces

An internal force is a force that acts from within the structure. Let us look at four types of internal forces.

Imagine that we start with a rectangular block of material.

Compression is a pushing force that squeezes a material. This force often makes materials shorter.

Example: Hold a soft sponge flat in the palm of one hand. Push down on the top of the sponge with your other hand. You are creating compression.

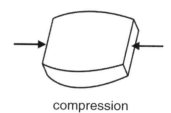

compression

Tension is a pulling force that stretches a material. This force often makes materials longer.

Example: Hold one end of an elastic band in each hand. Move your hands farther apart. You are creating tension that stretches the elastic band.

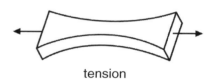

tension

Torsion is a twisting or turning force.

Example: To wring out a wet washcloth, you use the twisting force of torsion. You hold the washcloth in two hands and twist it in opposite directions to force out the water.

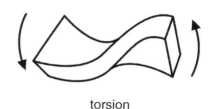

torsion

Bending is a force that makes a straight material curved. One side of the material squeezes together (compression). The other side stretches apart (tension).

Example: A soft or damp sponge is easy to bend. Hold it in both hands and bend it in the same way as shown in the diagram. Tension acts on the top side and compression acts on the bottom side.

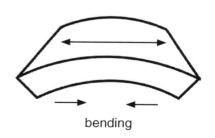

bending

"Four Types of Internal Forces"—Think About It!

Identify the internal force at work in each of the examples below. Explain your thinking.

1. Ling loves sleeping on her new mattress. Her old mattress was as hard as a board. The new mattress sinks comfortably under her when she climbs into bed.

   What type of internal force acts on the mattress when she lies on it? _____

   _____

   _____

2. Rick tunes his guitar. Rick tightens a guitar string to make it play in tune. To tighten it, he turns the tuning peg at the end of the guitar string.

   a) What type of internal force acts on the guitar string? _____

   _____

   _____

   b) What type of internal force acts on the tuning peg?

   _____

   _____

3. Maria and her brother Marco are making a fall wreath for their door. The first step is to take a straight piece of wire and make it into a circle.

   What type of internal force acts on the wire as they make it into a circle? _____

   _____

   _____

4. Mr. Green is fishing and a big fish has taken the bait. The fish tries to swim away as Mr. Green tries to reel it in.

   What type of internal force acts on the fishing line? _____

   _____

   _____

   _____

Experimenting with Materials and Forces

How do different materials withstand internal forces? Try this experiment to find out.

What You Need

- Wooden craft stick
- Sponge
- Eraser
- Plastic straw
- New, unsharpened wooden pencil

What You Do

1. Read the rating scale at the bottom of this page.

2. Predict how well each material will withstand each force. Use the rating scale to make your predictions. Record your predictions in the results chart on the next page.

3. Test how well each material withstands tension. Pull on each material from both ends. Use the rating scale for each material and record the results in the chart.

4. Test how well each material withstands compression. Push on each material from both ends. Use the rating scale for each material and record the results in the chart.

5. Test how well each material withstands torsion. Twist each end in a different direction. Use the rating scale for each material and record the results in the chart.

6. Test how well each material withstands bending. Press down on each end with your fingers. Press up in the middle with your thumbs. (Do not waste classroom materials! See if the pencil will bend without using enough force to break it.) Use the rating scale for each material and record the results in the chart.

Rating Scale		
1	**Weak:** A very small amount of force makes the material change shape or break.	
2	**Fair:** A small amount of force makes the material change shape or break.	
3	**Good:** A lot of force makes the material change shape or break.	
4	**Very Strong:** A lot of force makes no change or very little change in the material's shape.	

"Experimenting with Materials and Forces"—Think About It!

Use the chart below and the rating scale on page 29 to record your predictions and results.

Material	Tension	Compression	Torsion	Bending
Wooden craft stick	Prediction: _____ Result: _____	Prediction: _____ Result: _____	Prediction: _____ Result: _____	Prediction: _____ Result: _____
Sponge	Prediction: _____ Result: _____	Prediction: _____ Result: _____	Prediction: _____ Result: _____	Prediction: _____ Result: _____
Eraser	Prediction: _____ Result: _____	Prediction: _____ Result: _____	Prediction: _____ Result: _____	Prediction: _____ Result: _____
Plastic straw	Prediction: _____ Result: _____	Prediction: _____ Result: _____	Prediction: _____ Result: _____	Prediction: _____ Result: _____
Pencil	Prediction: _____ Result: _____	Prediction: _____ Result: _____	Prediction: _____ Result: _____	Prediction: _____ Result: _____

Below, record any notes about your results or any questions you wonder about.

_____

_____

_____

_____

_____

_____

_____

_____

_____

Forces and Shapes

Strong shapes are used when people design buildings. These shapes make buildings that can withstand the forces that act on them. Three strong shapes are often used in buildings. These shapes are rectangles, arches, and triangles.

In the diagrams below, the pairs of arrows show the following forces at work:

← → tension   → ← compression

Rectangles

A rectangle can be quite strong. But it is not as strong when a force pushes on one of the vertical sides. Its shape can change, making it weaker. Builders add a diagonal support piece to make the rectangle stronger. This support piece is called a brace. It goes between two opposite corners of the rectangle.

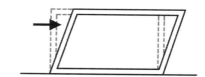

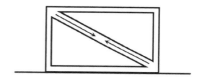

Arches

An arch is a strong shape. But it is not as strong when a force pushes down on the top of the arch. When a force pushes down on the top of the arch, the sides of the arch spread outward. To make an arch stronger, builders add supports on each side. These supports are called buttresses. The buttresses prevent the sides of the arch from spreading outward.

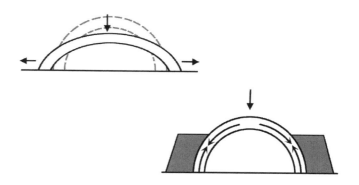

Triangles

A triangle can be a very strong shape. If a force pushes on the top point, the triangle is very strong. But if a force pushes on the side of a triangle, the side can bend.

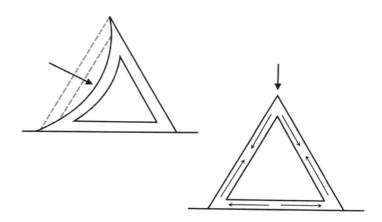

"Forces and Shapes"—Think About It!

1. A pushing force is applied to the side of a rectangle. What internal force acts on the brace?

_____

2. A force pushes down on the top point of a triangle.

a) What internal force acts on the two sloping sides of a triangle?

_____

b) What internal force acts on the bottom of the triangle?

_____

3. Some houses have a sloped roof that forms a triangle. The top point of the triangle does not support any weight. But the sloping sides are useful in areas where it rains and snows.

a) What might happen to a flat roof if a storm brings a lot of snow? Why?

_____

_____

b) Which roof would be safer for a house built in an area that gets a lot of snow: a triangular roof or a flat roof? Why?

_____

_____

c) A triangular roof is not easily damaged by rain. Why?

_____

_____

4. a) What two shapes are used to build an igloo?

_____

b) You have built an igloo and you know that a heavy snowfall is coming. How could you make the igloo's entrance strong enough to support the weight of the snow? (Snow is the only material you have to work with.)

_____

_____

Four Types of Bridges

In the diagrams below, the pairs of arrows show the following forces at work:

← → tension   → ← compression

Beam Bridge

A beam bridge has a horizontal beam supported by two piers. The beam bends when a load is on the bridge. A load can be cars, trucks, or a train. Compression acts on the top side of the beam. Tension acts on the bottom side of the beam.

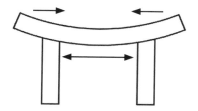

Arch Bridge

The arch is a very strong shape. A load on top of the bridge causes compression on the top of the bridge. It also causes tension along the arch underneath the bridge. This tension could cause the arch to spread apart, making it weaker. The material on the sides of the arch acts like buttresses. The material keeps the arch from spreading apart.

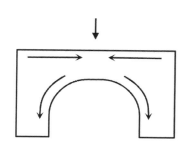

Truss Bridge

A truss bridge is built with triangles made of steel bars. A triangle is a very strong shape. Compression and tension forces act on the bridge. The diagram below shows the forces.

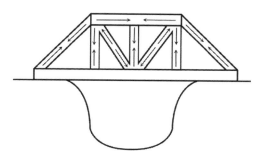

Suspension Bridge

On a suspension bridge, tall towers support the main cable. Smaller cables attached to the main cable support the roadway. These cables are called suspenders. The main cable is attached to large blocks at each end of the bridge. The load of traffic on the bridge is transferred to the suspenders. This causes tension in the suspenders. The suspenders transfer the load to the main cable. This causes tension in the cables. Compression acts on the towers as they support the weight of the bridge and the traffic.

1. Snow and ice can build up on the roadway of a bridge, making it heavier. Are snow and ice internal or external forces? Explain your answer.

_____

_____

_____

_____

2. A simple beam bridge can be built over a stream. All you need are two blocks and a wooden plank.

   a) What force acts on the blocks when someone is crossing the bridge?

_____

_____

   b) What force (or forces) will act on the plank?

_____

_____

   c) Is the weight of the plank an internal or external force?

_____

_____

3. You are designing a bridge that will take tour buses to an interesting place. Explain why you would need to know the following information:

   a) The maximum number of people that can fit in one bus

_____

_____

   b) The maximum number of buses that can fit on the bridge

_____

_____

_____

Plastic Straw Bridge Challenge

Build a bridge out of straws that holds as much weight as possible.

What You Need

- Plastic straws
- Masking tape
- Scissors
- 100 nickels in a plastic cup
- 2 desks of equal height

What You Do

1. Sketch out a design of a bridge before building it.
2. You can only use scissors to cut the straws.
3. You can only use masking tape to hold the bridge together.
4. The bridge should span two desks 100 cm apart.
5. Once complete, test the bridge by seeing how many nickels it can hold.

Think About It!

1. Sketch a drawing of your bridge on a separate piece of paper.
2. Predict how many nickels you think your bridge will hold. _____
3. What happened when you added nickels to test your bridge?

_____

_____

_____

4. How many nickels can your bridge hold? _____
5. What are some ways to improve your design?

_____

_____

_____

Try this challenge using another material such as spaghetti!

The Incredible Chunnel

It took more than six years, required 13 000 workers, and cost $15 billion. Building the Channel Tunnel (often called the "Chunnel") was one of the largest engineering projects ever. It is 31.4 km long, and in places it lies as deep as 76 m below sea level.

The Digging Begins

The English Channel is a body of water that lies between southern England and northern France. The Chunnel runs under the English Channel and provides a link between England and France. In 1988, construction began in both countries. The project involved digging three tunnels. Two of the tunnels are for passenger trains and freight trains. These tunnels are each 7.6 m across. The other tunnel, which is just 5 m across, is a service tunnel that workers use for maintenance and to monitor the tunnels to ensure they stay safe.

Map of the Chunnel

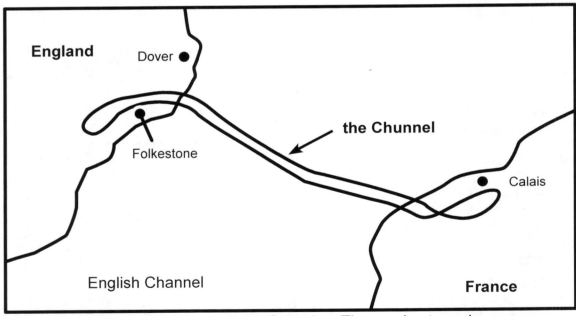

This map shows only the two tunnels for trains. The service tunnel runs between the two train tunnels.

How was it possible to dig such large tunnels? Workers used huge tunnel-boring machines (TBMs), which are also called "moles." At the front of each TBM is a large disc that has teeth

continued next page 👉

made of tungsten, a very hard metal. The disc rotates to break up the rock as the TBM slowly moves forward. Behind each TBM, a conveyor belt carries away the broken rock. Thanks to TBMs, Chunnel workers were able to dig about 76 m of a tunnel each day.

Chunnel Challenges

The weight of ocean water presses heavily on the tunnels. What keeps the tremendous weight of the water from collapsing the tunnels? As each section of a tunnel was dug, the sides were lined with concrete to make the tunnels strong. The lining also helps make the tunnels waterproof.

Since TBMs started digging in both France and England at the same time, how could engineers make sure that both parts of a tunnel would meet at the same spot in the middle? Solving this problem was one of the biggest challenges of the Chunnel project. Using special lasers and other equipment, workers from the two countries carefully dug toward each other. But the Chunnel was such a huge project that no one knew for sure if the tunnels really would meet at the same spot.

Construction of the service tunnel happened first. On December 1, 1990, the two sides of this tunnel successfully connected with each other. What a relief! A British worker and a French worker shook hands through the opening. Near the end of May 1991, both ends of the second tunnel were joined. About a month later, the two sides of the third tunnel met in the middle.

There was still lots of work to do. Train tracks, electrical systems, fireproof doors, a ventilation system, and more had to be added. As well, train terminals (stations) needed to be built in England and France at the ends of the Chunnel.

To remove any water that got into the tunnel system, three pumping stations were built under the water, as well as one on the British shore and one on the French coast. A special vehicle was designed to zoom along the service tunnel. This vehicle is used for maintenance on the Chunnel, and can quickly reach the site of an accident or emergency.

The Chunnel officially opened on May 6, 1994.

The Chunnel Today

As many as 400 trains pass through the Chunnel daily. More than 21 million passengers take the 35-minute train trip between the two countries each year. An organization of American engineers has included the Chunnel on its list of "Seven Wonders of the Modern World."

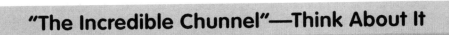

"The Incredible Chunnel"—Think About It

1. Making sure that the two ends of a tunnel connected in the middle was a difficult challenge. This problem could have been avoided if one TBM drilled a tunnel right across the English Channel. Why do you think the planners decided to have two TBMs start drilling at opposite ends of a tunnel?

_____

_____

_____

_____

_____

2. The map shows that the two tunnels for trains are connected at each end, forming a large loop. What problem would the Chunnel designers need to solve if the two tunnels could not be joined to create a loop?

_____

_____

_____

_____

_____

3. Some people involved in the Chunnel worked mostly in offices, designing the Chunnel and planning how it could be built. Other people worked right in the tunnels as they were being built. Which type of job would you prefer? Why?

_____

_____

_____

_____

Watch Out for Wind!

Nature's Forces

Some of the external forces that affect structures come from nature. When snow and ice build up on a structure, they add weight. The structure must be able to support that weight. An earthquake is an external force that occurs when large sections of Earth's crust start to move. These sections are called tectonic plates. This movement causes the ground to shake. The shaking can make structures such as buildings collapse.

Hurricanes and Tornadoes

Wind is another of nature's forces. Strong winds push against structures. The force of the wind can damage or destroy structures such as homes. Tornadoes and hurricanes have very strong winds. These winds can cause severe damage. Some people live in areas where these storms often happen. They must find ways to make their homes withstand the force of strong wind.

Protecting Structures from Wind

Strong wind can push against windows, causing them to shatter. Some people nail pieces of plywood over the windows to protect them.

A very strong wind can have enough force to lift the roof off a house. The structure of the house is much weaker once the roof is gone. The house may collapse. Some people use hurricane ties to attach the roof more securely to the house. Hurricane ties are strips of steel. They can withstand much more force than the nails that join the roof to the house.

Because of the threat of hurricanes or tornados, some buildings are made from different materials. They are not made from wood or bricks. Instead, they are built from reinforced concrete. Reinforced concrete has steel bars running through it. This material can withstand very strong winds.

Wind Makes Waves

Hurricanes form over oceans and they sometimes move over land. Hurricane winds can cause large waves. These waves can damage houses built along the ocean shore. One way to protect a house from wave damage is to build the house above the ground. Steel, concrete, or wood is used to create pillars. These pillars are called pilings. The house is built on top of the pilings so waves can travel under the house without damaging it.

1. When strong winds become dangerous, people often seek shelter in a basement. Why is a basement a good place to go?

_____

_____

_____

2. During a hurricane or tornado, people are told to go to a safe place in their home. They are also told to cover themselves with a heavy blanket. Why might they use a blanket?

_____

_____

_____

3. A special type of nail can be used for building homes. One feature of this nail is that it has rings that create sharp points. (See the cross-section diagram.) Do you think this nail would help wooden structures to survive a hurricane or tornado? Why?

_____

_____

_____

_____

4. People look for new ideas for creating safer homes in hurricane areas. One idea is to make houses in the shape of a dome. Do you think a house built in this shape would be less likely to be damaged in a hurricane? Why?

_____

_____

_____

_____

_____

_____

Earthquake!

Earthquakes are frightening events that can injure or kill people and cause incredible damage to structures. Scientists have developed technology to detect earthquakes so that people can be alerted as soon as an earthquake starts.

What Causes an Earthquake?

An earthquake is the shaking of Earth's surface. There are many huge rocky plates under Earth's surface, and these plates continually move very slowly past one another. As the plates move, they put pressure on themselves and on each other. If the pressure becomes strong enough, the plates crack. This crack is called a fault.

When a fault is created, the pressure on the plates turns into waves of energy that move through the ground, making it shake. The area around the fault experiences an earthquake.

The focus of an earthquake is the place where the underground plates first start to crack. The epicentre of an earthquake is the part of Earth's surface that is directly above the focus.

More than one million earthquakes happen each year, but many cause only gentle shaking. Some earthquakes take place in areas where there are few people or human-built structures. These earthquakes do not cause much harm. When an earthquake happens in a place where many people live, the effects can be devastating.

How Do Scientists Detect and Measure Earthquakes?

Scientists use instruments called seismometers (size-MAWM-i-ters) to measure the motion of Earth's surface. *Seismo* comes from a Greek word that means "shaking," and *meter* is a Greek word that means "to measure." Seismometers can detect the beginning of an earthquake, measure how strong it is, and measure how long it lasts.

A seismometer uses electronic sensors to detect the shaking of the ground during an earthquake. When a seismometer detects that an earthquake is happening, computers and alarms are used to warn people. The diagram on the next page shows a very simple seismometer that does not use electronic sensors. The seismometers that scientists use are much more complicated.

continued next page

A Simple Seismometer

The round weight stays in the same spot while the seismometer moves back and forth as the ground shakes.

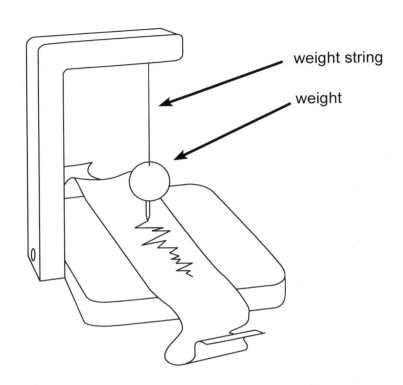

weight string

weight

The base of the seismometer and the arm the weight is attached to move back and forth as the ground shakes. The string allows the round weight to stay in the same position during the shaking, even though the rest of the seismometer is moving. A small pen-like device at the bottom of the weight draws a line that shows how much the seismometer and the ground are moving.

Why Are Emergency Alert Systems Important?

Seismometers can detect the very beginning of an earthquake, when the ground is moving so little that most people do not notice. At the first signs of an earthquake, alarms notify people to move to a safe place. There might very little time before the shaking becomes much stronger, but even a few seconds' warning can save lives. People might have time to duck under sturdy tables or safely stop their cars. In areas where earthquakes happen frequently, some hospitals, homes, offices, and classrooms have earthquake alarms installed.

What Do Seismologists Do?

Seismologists are scientists who study waves that travel through the ground. Some seismologists study earthquakes and try to predict when and where earthquakes will happen. These seismologists might also study the effects of earthquakes, such as tsunamis and landslides. Other seismologists study active volcanoes to watch for signs that one might be about to erupt.

"Earthquake!"—Think About It!

1. Review the diagram of the seismometer and the text that explains how it works. In your own words, explain how the pen-like device attached to the round weight can draw a zigzag line on the paper if the weight does not change position during an earthquake.

_____

_____

_____

_____

_____

_____

2. Imagine you are standing near train tracks when a train goes by. (Do not try this—stay away from moving trains!) You will probably feel vibrations in your body. Use information from the article to explain why you feel vibrations from the train.

_____

_____

_____

_____

_____

_____

3. Some seismologists try to predict when an active volcano will erupt. Based on information in the article, how might seismologists do this?

_____

_____

_____

_____

_____

_____

Protect Yourself!

Playing sports can be lots of fun, and the exercise is very good for you. But playing sports can also cause injuries. It is important to protect yourself with the proper safety equipment.

Forces and Sports

In many sports, the players, as well as things such as balls and pucks, all move fast. In baseball, the pitcher throws the ball at a high speed. A ball moving at high speed is harder to hit. The pitcher's throw is a pushing force. That force sends the ball speeding toward the batter. The batter uses a pushing force to swing the bat. When the bat hits the ball, it changes the direction of the ball. The bat sends the ball sailing into the outfield. A ball that is moving quickly has a large amount of force. When the ball comes in contact with a person, the force is transferred to the person's body. Without safety equipment, this force can cause serious injuries.

Players also move quickly in many sports. The players use their legs to create a pushing force that moves them forward. In some sports, players can move *very* fast. A hockey player can race down the ice faster than a person can run. A person riding a skateboard can move extremely fast when going down a hill. (This is because of wheels and the force of gravity.) If a fast-moving player falls or crashes into something, they can be injured.

Sports Safety Equipment

Most sports safety equipment protects players in three ways:

- **Absorbing force:** Many types of safety equipment have foam padding. This absorbs some of the force of a speeding ball or puck. It can even protect them from another player. Less of the force is transferred to the player's body. This means there is less chance of a player being injured.
- **Spreading out force:** A puck moves very fast. If it hits you in the head, the force of the puck is transferred to your head. So a lot of force is transferred to the small part of your head the puck hits. A helmet will spread the puck's force over a larger area. This makes the force less intense in any one spot. This means you are less likely to be injured by the force. The foam padding inside a helmet will also absorb some of the force.
- **Protecting skin:** Scrapes and cuts are usually not serious injuries. But they can hurt and might become infected if not looked after properly. Safety equipment protects skin. An example is hockey skates made from thick leather. They are made to support and protect a player's feet and ankles. They also protect them from being cut by another player's skate blade.

"Protect Yourself!"—Think About It!

1. Hockey goalies wear thick leg pads. Other players do not wear the same type of leg pads. Why do goalies need extra protection for their legs?

_____

_____

_____

_____

2. a) How do the cushioned soles of running shoes protect runners?

_____

_____

_____

  b) Cushioned soles need to be able to withstand two internal forces: compression and bending. Explain why.

_____

_____

_____

_____

3. The foam padding inside a helmet is like a sponge. It can absorb the force of compression by becoming thinner. It is very important not to wear a helmet that fits too tightly. Explain why.

_____

_____

_____

_____

4. Skateboarders should crouch down on the skateboard if they are about to fall. Why? How would this help to protect skateboarders?

_____

_____

_____

_____

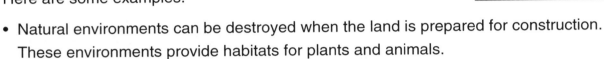

Structures and the Environment

Humans build many types of structures. They build office towers and shopping malls. They also build bridges, and steel towers that support electrical lines. All of these structures affect the environment.

Negative Effects of Structures

Building a structure can damage the environment. Here are some examples:

- Natural environments can be destroyed when the land is prepared for construction. These environments provide habitats for plants and animals.
- Building materials have to be brought to the site, sometimes from places far away. The trucks that bring the materials pollute the air. They also cause noise pollution.
- The materials used in construction can damage the environment. For example, steel is made from iron, which comes from mines. The stone used to create concrete comes from quarries. Mines and quarries damage the beauty of natural environments and create pollution.
- Materials such as iron and stone are turned into steel and concrete in large factories. These factories use a lot of energy and create pollution.

Positive Effects of Structures

Some of the structures people build have a positive effect on the environment.

- Bridges and boardwalks help protect fragile environments, such as marshes and sand dunes, that would be damaged by visitors' footsteps.
- Wind generators are giant windmills. They produce electricity from the force of the wind. Wind generators make little pollution. That is why they are sometimes called a source of "clean energy" or "green energy."
- What grows on a solar farm? Nothing! Solar farms are large areas covered with large structures called solar panels. These structures turn sunlight into electricity. They do not put any pollution into the air.
- Tunnels under roads let animals travel safely to other areas of their habitat without being hit by a car.

"Structures and the Environment"—Think About It!

1. Wind generators and bridges have positive effects on the environment. But it is impossible to create these structures without damaging the environment. List two ways in which creating these structures damage the environment.

_____

_____

_____

_____

2. Tina found out that a bridge will be built across the river near her town. She wonders if having a ferry take cars across the river would be better. A ferry would have these advantages for the environment:

   • Less construction equipment would be required at the site. This equipment can damage the natural landscape.
   • Producing the steel and concrete needed for the bridge will damage the environment. A ferry requires less material.

   List two ways in which a ferry could have *negative* effects on the environment.

_____

_____

_____

3. Tina's community holds a town hall meeting. They discuss whether a bridge or a ferry is the better solution. Which option do you think each of the following groups would choose? Explain why.

   a) Unemployed construction workers

_____

_____

   b) People who like to fish in the part of the river where the ferry would operate

_____

_____

Forces and Structures Quiz

Test your knowledge of forces and structures by answering the questions below.

1. A force can make an object change _____, _____, or

_____.

2. A ball is thrown straight up in the air. How does gravity affect its speed and direction?

_____

_____

3. Describe the difference between an external force and an internal force.

_____

_____

_____

4. Name each of the forces described below.

a) A twisting or turning force: _____

b) A force that makes a straight material become curved: _____

c) A pulling forces that stretches a material: _____

d) A pushing force that squeezes a material: _____

5. Draw two shapes that make structures stronger.

6. Sports safety equipment helps protect players from injury. List three types of protection sports safety equipment provides.

_____

_____

What Is Matter?

Everything you see around you is made of matter. Matter is anything that has mass and takes up space.

Mass and Volume

Mass is the amount of matter in an object. Matter is made up of tiny particles. Since every object is made of particles, every object has mass. The more particles an object has, the greater its mass is.

Volume is the amount of space that matter takes up. It is easy to see that different objects take up different amounts of space. A baseball takes up more space than a marble, so a baseball has greater volume than a marble.

Comparing Mass and Volume

If two objects have the same volume, do they have the same mass? Not necessarily. Remember that objects are made of matter, and matter is made of particles. Two objects that are the same size can be made up of different numbers of particles. Why? In some materials, the particles are packed more tightly together.

Imagine you have two solid blocks, one made of wood and one of steel. The blocks are exactly the same size, so they have the same volume. Do they have the same mass? No. The particles in steel are packed together more tightly than the particles in wood. So there are more particles in the steel block than in the wooden block. As you can probably guess, the block of steel would weigh more than the block of wood.

In the same way, two objects with the same mass might not have the same volume. One kilogram of wool takes up a lot more space than one kilogram of marbles. They have the same mass. But the particles in wool are more spread out.

Brain Stretch

Mass is measured on a scale. It measures the pull of gravity on your mass. If you travel to the Moon your mass will not change, but a scale on the Moon will say you weigh less. That is because the Moon's gravity does not pull as much as Earth's gravity.

1. Which of the following are made of matter? Put a check mark in the appropriate box.

a) Elephant	❑ Matter	❑ Not matter
b) Ping-pong ball	❑ Matter	❑ Not matter
c) Window glass	❑ Matter	❑ Not matter
d) Maple syrup	❑ Matter	❑ Not matter
e) Hair	❑ Matter	❑ Not matter
f) Fog	❑ Matter	❑ Not matter

2. You have two cubes, each made of a different material. One cube is slightly larger than the other.

    a) Circle the sentence that has to be true.

        A. The larger cube has more mass than the smaller cube.

        B. The smaller cube has less volume than the larger cube.

    b) Explain why two objects that have the same volume might not have the same mass.

_____

_____

_____

_____

_____

3. For each pair of objects, put a check mark beside the object that has the greater volume.

    a) ❑ a grapefruit ❑ a watermelon   b) ❑ a dime ❑ a quarter

4. Salima is doing an experiment to compare two objects. First, she fills two identical glasses with the same amount of water. When she drops the first object into a glass, the water level rises but the water does not overflow. When she drops the second object into the other glass, the water overflows.

    a) Which property of matter is Salima investigating: mass, volume, or both? _____

    b) Complete the sentence to tell what Salima learned about the objects.

    The second object has _____ than the first object.

Properties of Matter

What Are Properties?

Objects have different properties. Properties are characteristics that we can notice with our five senses, or characteristics that we can measure or test.

Types of Properties

You can easily tell the difference between a lemon and a lime because your sense of sight tells you that one is yellow and the other is green. Colour is a property. Mass and volume are two other properties of matter. You can measure these properties.

Solubility—how easily a substance dissolves in a liquid. If you put sand in a glass of water and stir, the sand will not dissolve. It is not soluble. If you put sugar in a glass of water and stir, the sugar will dissolve. Sugar is soluble. Some substances dissolve more easily than others.

Viscosity—how easily a substance flows. Imagine pouring a cup of milk and a cup of honey. Which will pour out first? The milk, of course! Viscosity is really about how much a substance *resists* flowing. Honey has higher viscosity than milk because honey resists flowing more than milk does.

Transparency—how well light passes through a substance. If the substance is clear (you can see objects through it), it is *transparent*. If light passes through the substance, but you cannot see objects through it, it is *translucent*. If no light passes through the substance, it is *opaque*.

Hardness—how easily an object changes shape. A hard object, such as a rock, does not change shape easily. A soft object, such as a pillow, changes shape easily. If you push down on a pillow—even with very little force—you will make a dent in it. The shape of the pillow has changed.

Why is it important to understand the properties of matter? People who design products consider the properties of the materials they use. For example, if you are going to make sponges or diapers, you will need to consider the absorbency of the materials you use. Materials and the products we make from them are all made of matter.

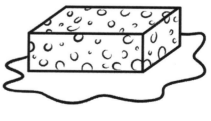

sponge

"Properties of Matter"—Think About It!

1. Bath towels and dish towels are usually made of cotton. Use two of the properties mentioned on the previous page to explain why cotton is a good material to use for towels.

   _____

   _____

   _____

   _____

2. It can take a while for ketchup to flow out of the bottle.

   a) Does this mean that ketchup has a high viscosity, or a low viscosity?

   _____

   b) Give three other properties of ketchup.

   _____

   _____

3. The plastic wraps that we use to keep food fresh are transparent. Why is the property of transparency useful in a plastic wrap?

   _____

   _____

   _____

4. Jim is inventing a new type of powdered drink that can be mixed with water. When he tested it out by mixing it in a glass of water, he found that the powder has low solubility. What did Jim see when he looked in the glass after adding the powder and stirring it?

   _____

   _____

5. Give four properties of your desk.

   _____

   _____

   _____

Experiment: Do All Liquids Dissolve in Water?

When people wash dishes by hand, they use a liquid dish detergent. The dish detergent does not sit in a glob in the bottom of the sink—it dissolves in the water. Try this experiment to see if all liquids dissolve in water.

What You Need

- Isopropyl alcohol (rubbing alcohol)
- Corn syrup
- Vegetable oil
- Water
- 6 clear plastic cups
- Masking tape
- 3 straws
- 5 mL measure
- 15 mL measure

SAFETY ALERT

Do **not** drink any of the liquids in this experiment.

What You Do

1. Use pieces of masking tape to label three of the cups with these labels: Alcohol, Corn Syrup, Vegetable Oil.

2. Use masking tape to create labels for the other three cups: Alcohol + Water, Corn Syrup + Water, Vegetable Oil + Water.

3. Pour 10 mL of alcohol into the cup with the appropriate label. (Use the cup with the label "Alcohol," **not** the cup labelled "Alcohol + Water.")

4. Pour 10 mL of corn syrup into the appropriate cup, and 10 mL of vegetable oil into the appropriate cup.

5. Pour 30 mL of water into each of the cups with "+ Water" on the label.

6. Pour the alcohol into the cup labelled "Alcohol + Water." Observe the cup from the side as you pour. Watch what happens and record your observations on the next page.

7. Stir the alcohol and water with a straw and see whether the alcohol seems to dissolve in the water. (Keep watching from the side.) Record your observations.

8. Repeat steps 6 and 7 for each of the other two liquids (corn syrup and vegetable oil) using a clean straw to stir each mixture. Make sure you pour each liquid into the correct cup. Record your observations after doing each step.

"Experiment: Do All Liquids Dissolve in Water?"—Think About It!

1. What did you observe when you poured alcohol into the water?

_____

_____

_____

2. What did you observe when you stirred the alcohol and water?

_____

_____

_____

3. What did you observe when you poured the corn syrup into the water?

_____

_____

_____

4. What did you observe when you stirred the corn syrup and water?

_____

_____

_____

5. What did you observe when you poured the vegetable oil into the water?

_____

_____

_____

6. What did you observe when you stirred the vegetable oil and water?

_____

_____

_____

7. What is your conclusion—do all liquids dissolve in water?

_____

_____

States of Matter

Anything that has mass and takes up space is matter. Matter can exist in three different states—solid, liquid, or gas. Each of these states has different properties.

Solids

A solid holds its shape. For example, a rock is a solid. If you put a rock in a box, the rock will not take on the shape of the box.

Solids have a definite volume. The volume of a solid does not change. (Remember that volume is the amount of space that matter takes up.) A solid always takes up the same amount of space.

Liquids

Liquids take on the shape of the container they are in. For example, a fishbowl and an aquarium have different shapes. When you pour water into each container, the water takes on the shape of the container.

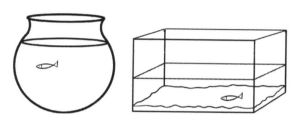

Liquids have a definite volume. Even though the shape of a liquid can change, it always takes up the same amount of space. Imagine that you fill a fishbowl with water. Then, you pour the water into an aquarium. The shape of the water changes, but its volume does not.

Gases

Most gases are invisible. We cannot see the air we breathe, but air is made up of different gases. When wind blows, we can feel these gases moving against our skin. Steam from a boiling kettle is a gas.

Gases do not have a definite shape. They take on the shape of the container they are in.

Gases do not have a definite volume. If you put a small amount of gas into a large container, the gas will spread out to fill the container.

Comparing Properties of Solids, Liquids, and Gases

Use the table to describe and compare the shape and volume of each state of matter.

State	Shape	Volume
Solid	- holds its shape	- has a definite volume
Liquid	- takes on the shape of its container	- has a definite volume
Gas	- takes on the shape of its container	- does not have a definite volume

"States of Matter"—Think About It!

1. Put each of the following in the correct column of the chart.

   - a drop of water
   - oxygen in the air
   - a pencil
   - an elastic band
   - ink in a marker
   - steam from hot soup
   - flowing lava

Solid	Liquid	Gas

2. While watching a science show on television, Jenny heard about a substance that expands to take up more space without changing from one state to another.

   Beside statements a) to c) write "True" or "False."

   a) The substance has a definite volume. _____

   b) The substance cannot be an example of matter. _____

   c) The substance could be either a liquid or a gas. _____

   d) Is the substance that Jenny heard about a gas, a liquid, or a solid? How do you know?

   _____

   _____

   _____

3. Rick gets on an empty elevator and smells perfume. When he crouches down low, the scent is just as strong as when he is standing.

   a) What is Rick smelling: a solid, a liquid, or a gas? _____

   b) Why is the scent just as strong when Rick is standing or crouching?

   _____

   _____

   _____

Experiment: What State Is It In?

Shaving foam is made of soap, but it is not hard like a bar of soap or runny like liquid soap. Can we classify shaving foam as a solid, liquid, or gas? Try the experiment below.

What You Need

- Paper towel
- Shaving foam (not shaving gel)
- Nickel
- Magnifying glass
- Ruler

What You Do

1. Place a blob of shaving foam on a piece of paper towel. Your blob of shaving foam should be roughly circular, about 4 to 5 cm in diameter, and about 3 cm high. Observe the shaving foam for a moment, then answer question 1.
2. Very gently lay the nickel flat on top of the shaving foam. Observe what happens and answer question 2. Then carefully remove the nickel.
3. Look at the shaving foam through a magnifying glass. Answer question 3.
4. Using your index finger, scoop up a little of the shaving foam. Rub it between your thumb and fingers and notice how it feels. Answer question 4.
5. Put the blob of shaving foam in a place where it will not be disturbed. Leave it for two or three days. Then observe any changes in how it looks and feels, and answer questions 5 and 6.

Think About It!

1. A solid keeps its shape when it is not in a container.
   a) Does the blob of shaving foam keep its shape? _____
   b) Would you say that shaving foam is a solid? Why or why not?

   _____

   _____

   _____

2. a) What happened when you put the nickel on top of the shaving foam?

   _____

   _____

b) Would you now say the shaving foam is a solid, a liquid, or a gas? Why?

_____

_____

_____

3. a) What did you observe when you looked at the shaving foam through a magnifying glass?

_____

_____

b) Based on what you saw, would you say that shaving foam is a solid, a liquid, or a gas?

_____

_____

4. a) How does the shaving foam feel when you rub it between your fingers?

_____

_____

b) Based on how the shaving foam feels on your fingers, what state would you say it is: a solid, a liquid, or a gas? _____

5. a) What changes do you notice after leaving the shaving foam for two or three days?

_____

_____

b) Based on what you observe, what state would you say the shaving foam is now: a solid, a liquid, or a gas? Why?

_____

_____

_____

6. Based on all your observations, what is shaving foam: a solid, a liquid, a gas, or something else? Explain your thinking.

_____

_____

_____

Changes in States of Matter

Matter can change from one state to another. For example, we can freeze a liquid to turn it into a solid. We can melt a solid to turn it into a liquid. We can boil a liquid to turn it into a gas. When matter changes state, heat is involved.

From Solid to Liquid: Melting

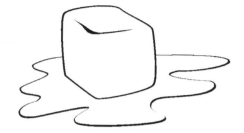

Melting is a process that changes a solid into a liquid. Solids melt when they absorb heat. An icicle melts when it absorbs heat from the air around it. An ice cube melts in a glass of water, even when the water is cold. Why? Cold water is warmer than an ice cube, so the ice cube can absorb heat from the water.

From Liquid to Gas: Evaporation

Evaporation is the process that changes a liquid into a gas. Liquids evaporate when they absorb heat. Steam coming out of a boiling kettle is water that has turned into a gas by evaporating.

From Gas to Liquid: Condensation

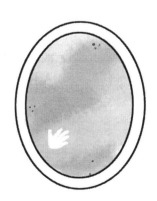

Condensation is the process that turns a gas into a liquid. Gases condense when they release heat. When you get out of a hot shower, the mirror in your bathroom may look misty or cloudy. This is caused by condensation. Some of the hot water from the shower evaporates, becoming water vapour (steam) in the air. The water vapour releases heat when it touches the mirror, which is cooler than the vapour. The vapour condenses into the tiny drops of water that cloud your mirror.

From Liquid to Solid: Freezing

Freezing is the process that changes a liquid into a solid. Water freezes when the air around it is cold enough. The cold air makes the water release heat. Why can you not make ice cubes in a refrigerator? The air in a refrigerator is not cold enough to make the water release enough heat to turn into ice. (The process of changing from a liquid to a solid is sometimes called *solidification*.)

continued next page

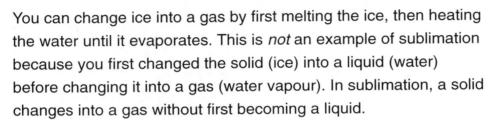

From Solid to Gas: Sublimation

Sublimation is the process that changes a solid into a gas. This change of state happens when the solid absorbs heat. Mothballs are small white balls with a strong odour that keeps moths away. (Moths like to eat certain types of material.) Over time, mothballs get smaller and smaller. That happens because mothballs contain chemicals that sublimate. The mothball does not change into a liquid before becoming a gas.

You can change ice into a gas by first melting the ice, then heating the water until it evaporates. This is *not* an example of sublimation because you first changed the solid (ice) into a liquid (water) before changing it into a gas (water vapour). In sublimation, a solid changes into a gas without first becoming a liquid.

From Gas to Solid: Deposition

Deposition is the process that changes a gas into a solid. This change of state happens when gas releases heat. Snowflakes are formed through deposition. When the air is cold enough, water vapour (a gas) in the air changes directly into ice (a solid) without becoming a liquid first. Deposition also creates the frost that forms on plants. When a leaf is cold enough, water vapour in the air changes state to become the ice we see on the leaf.

1. Complete as much as you can of the charts below without looking back at the article. Then review the article to find any information missing from your charts, and to correct any incorrect information.

	Changing from a...	Into a...	The process is called...
a)			Condensation
b)		Liquid	
c)	Solid		Sublimation
d)	Gas	Solid	
e)	Liquid	Gas	
f)			Freezing

	To change from a...	Into a...	Is heat absorbed or released?
g)	Solid	Liquid	
h)	Solid	Gas	
i)	Liquid	Solid	
j)	Liquid	Gas	
k)	Gas	Liquid	
l)	Gas	Solid	

2. For each process below, name the opposite process. For example, melting (changing a solid into a liquid) is the opposite of freezing (changing a liquid into a solid).

a) Condensation _____

b) Sublimation _____

c) Melting _____

Physical Changes and Chemical Changes

Changes in matter can be physical changes or chemical changes. Physical changes are reversible, and chemical changes are irreversible (cannot be reversed).

Physical Changes

Changes in states of matter are always physical changes because they can be reversed. For example, you can melt an ice cube (a solid), then freeze the water (a liquid) to turn it back into ice. Or, you can boil water to make it evaporate into water vapour (a gas), then cool the water vapour to make it condense into liquid water. In both examples, the substance—water—has not changed into something else. The water changes from one state to another, but it is still always water.

Changes in states of matter are not the only types of physical change. If you cut an apple into two pieces, you have changed the shape of the apple but both pieces are still apple. You can reverse the change by putting the two pieces back together.

Chemical Changes

In a chemical change, a new substance—or more than one new substance—is formed. The change is not reversible. For example, if you burn a piece of wood, two new substances are formed: smoke and ash. The smoke and ash cannot be turned back into wood. If you cook an egg, you cannot change the cooked egg back into a raw egg.

Signs of a Chemical Change

The following are signs that a chemical change is happening:

- **Change in colour:** When leaves change colour in autumn, they are going through a chemical change.
- **Change in odour:** You can tell that an egg is rotten because of the awful odour. A rotting egg is undergoing a chemical change.
- **A precipitate forms:** A precipitate is a solid that forms when certain liquids are mixed together. If you see a precipitate form, you know that a chemical change has happened.
- **A gas is produced:** When you mix certain substances together, the mixture will begin to bubble. The bubbles are made of a gas that is produced through a chemical change.

Identifying Physical and Chemical Changes

1. Cut out the cards below and arrange them in two columns—one for physical changes and one for chemical changes. Be prepared to explain your thinking.

PHYSICAL CHANGES	CHEMICAL CHANGES
Baking cookie dough	Molten lava hardening into rock
Bread becoming mouldy	Cooking rice
Lighting a match	Cracking open an egg
Crumpling tin foil	Digesting food
Breaking a glass	Toasting bread

Experiment: Observing a Chemical Change

Mixing substances together sometimes causes a chemical change to take place. This type of chemical change is called a chemical reaction. In this experiment, you can observe a chemical reaction.

What You Need

- Partner to work with
- Clean plastic water bottle (single-serving size)
- Water
- Effervescent antacid tablet
- Paper towel
- Latex balloon about 30 cm in diameter when inflated
- Clock or timer

SAFETY ALERT

Do **not** eat any of the antacid tablet or drink the liquid in this experiment.

Getting Ready

1. Blow up the balloon and let the air out. (Make sure the balloon does not get so big that it breaks.) Repeat two or three times.
2. Practice putting the opening of the balloon over the mouth of the water bottle. (You and your partner will need to do this fairly quickly during the experiment. Decide now who will hold the bottle steady and who will put the balloon over the mouth of the bottle.)

What You Do

3. Pour water into the bottle until the bottle is half full.
4. Over a paper towel, break the antacid tablet into several pieces. Drop the pieces into the bottle. (Be ready for the next step!)
5. Quickly put the balloon over the mouth of the bottle. Notice how the balloon looks.
6. Wait for one minute and watch what happens. (If the balloon gets big enough to break, do the next step right away.)
7. Pinch the neck of the balloon and carefully pull it off the bottle. Slowly let the air out of the balloon.
8. Pour the liquid down the drain and throw out the balloon.

1. Draw a picture that shows how the balloon looked when you first put it over the mouth of the bottle. Then draw what the balloon looked like after one minute.

2. Most gases are invisible. In this experiment, what are two signs that a gas is produced from a chemical change?

_____

_____

_____

_____

3. When the balloon expands, is it going through a chemical change or a physical change? Why do you think so?

_____

_____

_____

_____

What is happening in this experiment?

The antacid tablet contains chemicals that react with each other, causing a chemical change. These chemicals do not react with each other when they are dry (as in the tablet), but they do react with each other when they are dissolved in water. A new substance—carbon dioxide gas—forms from the chemical change that takes place.

Breakfast Science

Write a menu for the ultimate breakfast. Beside each menu item, indicate whether preparing the food involves a physical change (P), or a chemical change (C). Explain your thinking. Create a draft using the planner below. Create a good copy of your breakfast menu on a separate piece of paper.

_____'s Ultimate Breakfast Menu

Food item: _____

Type of Change:
Circle P or C

Describe the change

Food item: _____

Type of Change:
Circle P or C

Describe the change

Food item: _____

Type of Change:
Circle P or C

Describe the change

Food item: _____

Type of Change:
Circle P or C

Describe the change

What Is So Great About Gases?

Lots of inventions that people use every day rely on gases.

Air Bags in Cars

Air bags save lives and prevent injuries. An air bag inflates when it is filled with nitrogen gas. How does an air bag work? A car contains a crash sensor that can detect when a crash has taken place. The crash sensor sends a signal to the air bag's inflator. In the inflator, two chemicals react with each other in a chemical change that produces nitrogen gas. As the nitrogen gas starts to fill the air bag, the bag pops out and fully inflates. Tiny holes in the air bag allow the gas to escape so the passenger is not trapped behind the air bag.

An air bag has to inflate at lightning speed if it is going to prevent injury. Air bags burst out of their storage site at a speed of over 300 km/h. From the time a crash sensor detects a crash to when the air bag is fully inflated is only 1/25 of a second!

Aerosol Cans

Room fresheners and hairspray are available in aerosol cans, sometimes called spray cans. Gas is what makes aerosol cans work.

An aerosol can has gas at the top and the product (such as hairspray) at the bottom. The gas pushes down on the product. Since the product has nowhere to go, nothing happens. When you press the nozzle, you create an opening so the product has somewhere to go. The pushing force of the gas makes the product rush up a plastic tube. The product comes out of the nozzle in a spray.

nozzle

gas

plastic tube

product

The gas used in some aerosol cans is harmful to the environment. Many people choose products in a pump container instead.

Fire Extinguishers

Most fire extinguishers use a chemical foam or powder to put out fires. One type of extinguisher uses a gas to put out fires. The tank of this extinguisher is filled with liquid carbon dioxide. When the extinguisher is activated, the liquid carbon dioxide changes to a gas as it sprays out.

Fire needs oxygen. A fire will go out if not enough oxygen is available. Carbon dioxide gas pushes the oxygen away. The fire goes out because there is not enough oxygen around the fire to keep it burning.

"What Is So Great About Gases?"—Think About It!

1. An air bag needs to fill evenly with gas so that all parts of the air bag can protect passengers from injury. (If any part did not inflate as much, it would offer less protection from injury.) Explain why airbags always fill evenly.

_____

_____

_____

_____

_____

2. Since aerosol room fresheners can harm the environment, some people use air fresheners that are solids. Explain how solid air fresheners work. (**Hint:** Solid air fresheners work without melting.)

_____

_____

_____

_____

_____

_____

_____

_____

_____

Brain Stretch

Balloons filled with helium gas float because helium is lighter than air. Over time, a helium balloon will slowly deflate, even if the opening at the end of the balloon is tightly tied. Come up with a theory to explain why helium balloons deflate. Then do some research to find out whether your theory is correct. (**Hint:** The helium gas in the balloon does not change to another state inside the balloon.)

Changes of State Review

Under the diagram, write the name of the process indicated by each numbered arrow. Tell whether heat is absorbed or released in each process.

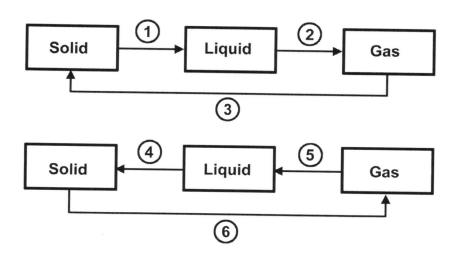

1. Process: _____

    Heat is _____ .

2. Process: _____

    Heat is _____ .

3. Process: _____

    Heat is _____ .

4. Process: _____

    Heat is _____ .

5. Process: _____

    Heat is _____ .

6. Process: _____

    Heat is _____ .

Matter Word Search

Solve each clue with one word. Then find the word in the word search puzzle.

1. Sublimation changes matter in this state into a gas. _____

2. The amount of space an object takes up. _____

3. When matter changes state, it is going through this type of change. _____

4. The term related to how easily a substance dissolves in liquid. _____

5. Matter in this state does not have a definite volume. _____

6. The amount of matter in an object. _____

7. The term related to how much a substance resists flowing. _____

8. This type of change in matter is not reversible. _____

Also look for these words related to the topic of matter:

liquid	particles	property	absorbency
dissolve	state	freeze	deposition

F	R	E	E	Z	E	V	Y	L	V	A	T	E
I	D	E	P	O	S	I	T	I	O	N	Y	U
Q	U	D	Y	G	O	S	I	P	L	D	C	L
P	T	I	W	O	Y	C	L	A	U	I	N	A
A	R	L	E	T	J	O	I	R	M	S	E	C
L	Y	O	M	A	S	S	B	T	E	S	B	I
G	A	S	P	A	T	I	U	I	D	O	R	M
S	T	A	T	E	O	T	L	C	X	L	O	E
E	O	U	K	M	R	Y	O	L	U	V	S	H
L	I	Q	U	I	D	T	S	E	R	E	B	C
E	C	A	F	D	P	H	Y	S	I	C	A	L

Natural Resources

Where did the paper this is printed on come from? What about the food you ate for breakfast, or the clothes you are wearing? Where does the electricity for the lights in your classroom come from? Everything that people use in their daily lives comes from Earth. We call these things natural resources because they come from nature. Some resources help us to stay alive. Others help us to live more enjoyable lives. Some are sources of energy.

Living and Non-living Resources

Natural resources can be living or non-living. Living things get energy from their environment to do things such as grow, move, and reproduce. A tree is a living thing. It uses water and sunlight to make energy so it can grow. A rock is a non-living thing. It does not use energy, and it does not grow or move on its own.

Fish are a very important living natural resource. Fish are a source of food for people. Water is a very important non-living natural resource. We use water for drinking, cooking, and washing. We also use water to make electricity. We use the electricity for energy to make many things work, such as the lights in our homes and schools.

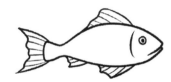

Renewable and Non-renewable Resources

Natural resources can also be renewable or non-renewable. Some renewable resources can be replaced or grown again. Trees are one example. Trees can reproduce themselves through seeds. Trees that are cut down can be replaced with seedlings. Seedlings are very young trees grown from seeds. Other renewable resources are always here for people to use. Wind is one example. Wind power is used to produce electricity.

Non-renewable resources cannot be replaced. They are non-renewable because they take a very long time to form. Fossil fuels and minerals are non-renewable resources. Oil is a fossil fuel. The oil we use today was formed millions of years ago. People use fossil fuels to produce energy. Oil can be made into gasoline to make cars and buses run.

"Natural Resources"—Think About It!

1. Complete the chart below with examples of living and non-living things. Try to list at least five for each category. Do not use examples from the text you have just read. Compare your chart with a classmate's chart. Do you agree with each other's examples?

Living Things	Non-living Things

2. Below is a list of natural resources. Beside each one, write whether it is renewable or non-renewable.

a) the Sun _____

b) coal _____

c) cotton plant _____

d) copper _____

e) salmon _____

f) cow _____

g) gasoline _____

h) ocean waves _____

3. Oil is used to make plastic bottles. Glass bottles are made from sand.

a) Which of these bottles could be called a renewable product? Why?

_____

_____

b) Which of these bottles is a non-renewable product? Why?

_____

_____

Using Resources

We use natural resources in many ways. We use some resources almost in their original form. We drink water and eat salmon. The water and the salmon are easy to identify. That is because they have not been changed into something else.

Products Made from Resources

Many resources are changed into products that we use. Sometimes it is easy to identify the resource that was used to make the product. Wood from trees is used to build houses and furniture. The wood in a bookcase looks like the wood in a tree. That is how we know it came from a tree. But wood can also be used to make paper, and paper does not look like wood.

Oil is a resource that is used in many different products. These include plastic containers, paint, soap, helmets, carpets, and tires. None of these look like the oil that comes from underground.

Different technologies are used to change resources into products. Before this can happen, the resources need to be harvested or extracted. Resources that are taken from Earth's surface are harvested. Resources that are taken from below Earth's surface are extracted. So trees are harvested, and oil is extracted.

From the Ground to Your Bathroom

Copper pipes are used for plumbing. You may have some copper pipes bringing water to the bathroom in your house. These are the steps for turning copper into copper pipes:

1. Ore containing copper is mined from below Earth's surface.
2. Ore is crushed, then ground into a powder.
3. The powder is concentrated so there is more copper in the mixture.
4. The copper mixture is smelted, or heated at high temperatures. This is done until it is 99 percent copper.
5. The copper is refined or made purer, then formed into big blocks.
6. Blocks are shipped to a manufacturer to make pipes.

That is one example of how we change a natural resource into a useful product.

"Using Resources"—Think About It!

1. Sometimes it is difficult to identify the resource a product was made from. Why?

_____

_____

2. a) Trees are harvested. Name two other resources that are harvested.

_____

b) Oil and copper are extracted. Name two other resources that are extracted.

_____

3. Copper ore and the copper used to make copper pipes are different. In what ways?

_____

_____

4. Below are the steps used to turn trees into the type of paper used in textbooks. Write the steps in the correct order in the flow chart.

- Bark is rubbed off the trees.
- Paper is coated to make finished paper.
- Logs are cut into chips.
- Paper is cut into sheets and packaged.
- Pulp is dried and pressed to make paper.
- Trees are cut down.
- Chips are cooked with chemicals to make pulp.
- Pulp is bleached to make it white.

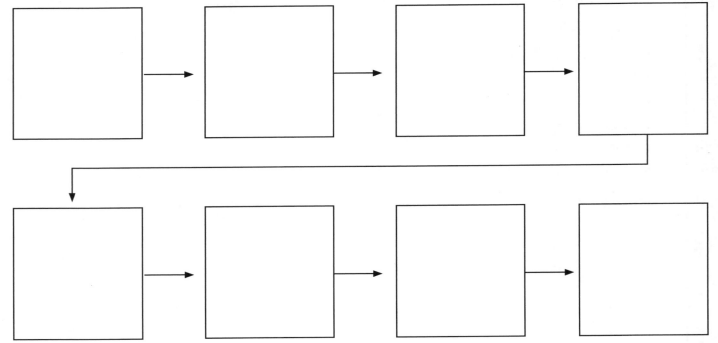

Conserving Resources

Conservation means using Earth's resources wisely and not wasting them. If people use resources too quickly, those resources might disappear. That means they will not be here for others to use in the future. Many governments, companies, and organizations now understand how important conservation is. So do people just like you. They try to do what they can to conserve resources.

People today are not the first to care about how Earth's resources are used. Aboriginal peoples in Canada have practised conservation for a long time.

Traditional Aboriginal Cultures

Most traditional Aboriginal people believed that they were the caretakers of Earth. They believed that everything on Earth was connected. This meant that all things had to be treated properly or other things would be affected. For example, if all the rabbits in an area were killed, this would affect other animals. Animals that ate rabbits, such as foxes, would probably leave the area. Plants that the rabbits ate would grow more and take over other plants. The area could change in many ways because there were no more rabbits.

So Aboriginal people took only the resources that they needed. They were also careful about how they took these resources. The First Nations people of the Kluane region in Yukon were hunters. They used all parts of the animals they killed. Most of the animal was eaten. The antlers of large animals such as moose were made into tools, spoons, knives, and needles. People tanned the animal hides, which changed the hides into leather. They used the hides and furs to make clothing and shelters. Hides that were not tanned were used to make snowshoes and hunting bags. They even used the animals' intestines and bladders to make containers for cooking and storage.

Anishinabe Culture

Many Anishinabe people lived in the forest areas of Ontario, where they hunted and gathered food. They moved a number of times during the year to find food and to follow food sources. But they also moved around to make sure they did not use up all the food in one area. Most of the year, the Anishinabe lived in small bands. But during the warmer months of the year, they gathered in larger groups for a while. During that time, they celebrated the end of winter and saw old friends and made new friends. The Anishinabe then moved on again. They stayed in places where they found fish, berries, and wild rice to live on but they never stayed for very long.

"Conserving Resources"—Think About It!

1. Three things that you can do to conserve resources are reduce, reuse, and recycle. By reducing, you use fewer resources and produce less garbage. When you reuse, you use the same product again or use it in a different way. Recycling is the third way to conserve. Many products can be recycled and made into new products. This includes things such as cans, paper, and glass.

In the chart below, list what you could do to conserve resources. Try to list three ideas for each column. Put a check mark beside the things that you already do.

I can reduce by...	I can reuse by...	I can recycle by...

2. How would using all parts of an animal help conserve resources? _____

_____

_____

3. How would moving from place to place during a year help conserve resources?

_____

_____

_____

4. Aboriginal people believe that everything on Earth is equal and important. So humans are equal to the forest, animals, and other parts of nature, not more important. How is this different from the way most people think today?

_____

_____

_____

Forms of Energy

Energy is the ability to do work. We use energy in everything we do. Our bodies use energy to grow. Cars use energy to move. Stoves use energy to cook food. Energy comes in many forms. Here are some examples:

- Chemical energy is energy that is stored in certain substances. Wood has chemical energy. When we burn wood, it releases its chemical energy.
- Motion energy or mechanical energy is motion that does work. Wind has motion energy. When wind moves, it can turn a windmill.
- Thermal energy is heat energy. We use heat energy to warm our homes.
- Electrical energy is movement, light, heat, or sound caused by electricity. Lightning is an example of electrical energy in nature. Electrical energy makes light bulbs work.

Sources of Energy

We get energy from different sources. Some of these sources are renewable. Renewable sources can be replaced or grown again. Examples of renewable sources include wind and trees. Here are some examples of energy from renewable sources:

- Biomass is energy from burning plants or garbage.
- Geothermal energy is heat energy from below Earth's surface.
- Hydroelectricity is energy from moving water.
- Solar energy is energy from the Sun.
- Wind energy is energy from wind.

We use renewable energy sources mainly to make electricity.

Most of our sources of energy are non-renewable. Non-renewable sources cannot be replaced because they take a very long time to form. Non-renewable sources include oil, natural gas, and coal. We use these sources mainly to produce electricity, heat, and gasoline. Oil, coal, and natural gas are fossil fuels. This means they were formed millions of years ago.

"Forms of Energy"—Think About It!

1. Read the examples below. Beside each one, write the form of energy the example shows: chemical, motion, thermal, or electrical.

   a) Throwing a bowling ball at the pins: _____

   b) Water falling over a dam: _____

   c) A battery in a flashlight: _____

   d) Turning on a gas fireplace: _____

   e) A computer plugged into a wall outlet: _____

2. Why are the Sun, wind, and moving water considered to be renewable energy sources?

   _____

   _____

3. Why are fossil fuels non-renewable energy sources?

   _____

   _____

4. Do you think wind energy could be an important source of energy everywhere in the world? Why or why not?

   _____

   _____

5. Why do you think fossil fuels are our main sources of energy?

   _____

   _____

Word Stretch

The prefix *bio* in biomass means "life." The prefix *geo* in geothermal means "earth" or "ground." The prefix *hydro* in hydroelectricity means "water." Find other words that start with each of these prefixes. What is the connection between each prefix and the meaning of each word?

Fossil Fuels

The three main fossil fuels are coal, oil, and natural gas. All of these were formed hundreds of millions of years ago, before the time of the dinosaurs.

When fossil fuels were formed, much of Earth was covered with swamps. The swamps were filled with trees, ferns, and other large leafy plants. The trees and plants died and sank to the bottom of the swamps. There they formed a spongy material called peat. Over many hundreds of years, sand, clay, and other minerals covered the peat. It slowly turned into rock. More and more rock was formed. The rock weighed down on the peat, squeezing all the water out of it. Over millions of years, the peat turned into coal, oil, and natural gas.

Oil also formed in the oceans. The ocean was full of tiny sea creatures called diatoms. When these creatures died, they fell to the sea floor where they were slowly covered by rock. Over time, heat and pressure turned them into oil.

Where Are Fossil Fuels Found Today?

Several countries in the Middle East are among the world's largest oil producers. Canada, the United States, Russia, and China are also among the largest oil-producing countries. Oil is found on land, as well as in the oceans. Canada has a number of drilling platforms in the ocean off the coast of Newfoundland.

The largest reserves of coal are found in the United States, Russia, and China. Canada is a mid-sized coal producer. British Columbia produces about one third of Canada's coal.

Natural gas is usually found with oil or coal. There may also be many undiscovered fossil fuel reserves in the world.

How We Use Fossil Fuels

One of the main uses of fossil fuels is to make electricity. In the world, coal is the main fuel source for making electricity. Natural gas and oil are also used.

The second main use of fossil fuels is to make fuels for vehicles. These fuels are mainly made from oil.

The third main use for fossil fuels is for heating and cooking in homes and businesses. Oil and natural gas are the main fuels used for these purposes.

"Fossil Fuels"—Think About It!

1. In the space below, make a flow chart to show how fossil fuels were formed.

2. Drills are used to get oil and natural gas from below Earth's surface. They make holes in the land or in the ocean floor. The oil or gas is then pumped out. Do you think it would be easier to drill on land or on the ocean floor? What are some problems that ocean drilling might present?

_____

_____

_____

_____

_____

3. Natural gas has no odour. It is highly combustible, which means it burns easily. Before the gas is delivered for use, a chemical is added to give it an odour. Why do you think this is done?

_____

_____

_____

_____

How We Use Energy

Canada is a very developed country. We use a lot of energy in our homes, schools, businesses, and for transportation. The government of Canada measures how much energy is used in four areas:

- Residential—This includes houses and apartments
- Commercial/Institutional—This includes buildings such as offices, stores, malls, hospitals, and schools
- Industrial—This includes buildings and equipment used for industries: examples of industries are manufacturing, construction, agriculture, mining, and forestry
- Transportation—This includes all vehicles that move people or goods: examples include cars, buses, trucks, and trains

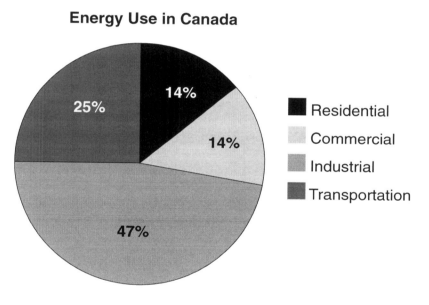

Energy Use in Canada

- Residential
- Commercial
- Industrial
- Transportation

The circle graph shows approximately how much energy is used in each of these areas.

Energy Use in Our Homes

In Canada, natural gas and electricity are used to heat most homes, including apartment buildings. About 20 percent of all homes are heated through the use of other fuels such as oil, wood, wood pellets, or propane. We also use energy in our homes for other purposes, including

- lighting
- heating water
- appliances such as refrigerators and blenders
- electronic equipment such as televisions and computers

The amount of electricity we use in our homes is increasing every year.

"How We Use Energy"—Think About It!

1. Why do you think industry uses so much energy?

_____

_____

_____

_____

2. Some people use wood or propane to heat their homes. Where do you think these people might live? Why might they use these fuels instead of natural gas or electricity?

_____

_____

_____

_____

3. People use more energy in their homes today than they did 20 years ago. What might have caused this increase in energy use?

_____

_____

_____

_____

4. In which room of your home does your family use the most energy? Why?

_____

_____

_____

_____

How Does Energy Work?

You have learned that energy is the ability to do work. You have also learned that energy comes in many forms. Each form of energy is either kinetic or potential. Kinetic energy is the energy of something moving, such as waves, rays, objects, electrons, atoms, molecules, and substances. So blowing wind is kinetic energy. It is also motion or mechanical energy. Potential energy is stored energy. So a battery has potential energy as well as chemical energy.

One very important thing about energy is that it cannot be created or destroyed. So when we use energy, it does not disappear. It just changes from one form of energy to another. An example is when a car engine burns gasoline. The engine changes the chemical energy of the gasoline into motion energy. The motion energy makes the car run. Some of the chemical energy is also changed into thermal energy. That is why a car engine heats up. The chemical energy from the gasoline has been changed to motion energy and thermal energy.

Energy Transformations

When energy changes from one form to another, we call it energy transformation. Here are some examples of energy transformations and their uses:

- A television changes electrical energy into sound and light energy. As a result, you can see and hear the television shows.
- A flashlight battery changes chemical energy into light energy. As a result, you can use the flashlight to see in the dark.
- A phone changes sound energy from your voice into electrical energy. This electrical energy is then changed back into sound energy. As a result, the person on the other end of the phone can hear what you said.
- Solar panels change sunlight into electric energy.

Energy transformations produce useful energy (energy that does work). They also produce wasted energy (usually as heat or sound). Most energy transformations are not very efficient. This means they produce a lot of wasted energy. For example, your body changes the chemical energy in food to motion energy. This gives you the energy to move, breathe, and think. But your body is not very efficient at converting food into useful energy. Your body is less than 5 percent efficient most of the time. The rest of the energy is lost as heat.

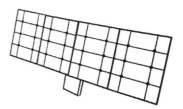

solar panel

"How Does Energy Work?"—Think About It!

1. Energy transformations make devices work so they can do things that help us. The alarm clock that wakes you up in the morning uses energy transformation. So does the bicycle you ride to school. Now it is your turn to design a device that will do a specific task. Your device can be something real, such as a child's toy. Or it can be something imaginary, such as a device that turns the pages of a book.

   Here are some guidelines:

   • You will not have to build the device, only design and sketch it.
   • Your device must have at least one energy transformation.
   • Your device must use materials that are readily available.

   On another sheet of paper, draw your design. Then answer the following questions:

   a) What is your device designed to do? _____

   _____

   b) Write a list of steps, in order, that explain how your device works. _____

   _____

   _____

   _____

   _____

   c) What energy transformation (or transformations) that will happen? When will it happen?

   _____

   _____

   d) Was any energy wasted in your device? What type of energy was wasted? Where was it lost?

   _____

   _____

   _____

   Share your design with a classmate. Talk about any improvements you could make to the device to make it work better.

Sources of Energy Brochure

Create a brochure on sources of energy!

STEP 1: Plan Your Brochure

☐ Take a piece of paper and fold the paper the same way your brochure will be folded. Before writing the brochure, plan the layout in pencil. Sections of the brochure should include
  • Descriptions of two types of renewable energy
  • Descriptions of two types of non-renewable energy
  • Advantages and disadvantages of each type of energy
  • How people use each type of energy
  • Interesting facts

☐ Write the heading for each section where you would like it to be in the brochure.

☐ Plan where graphics or pictures will be placed in the brochure.

STEP 2: Complete a Draft

☐ Research information for each section of your brochure. Check your facts.

☐ Read your draft for meaning, then add, delete, or change words to make your writing better.

☐ Plan what illustrations or graphics you will put into your brochure.

STEP 3: Checklist

☐ My brochure is neat and well organized.

☐ My brochure has accurate information.

☐ My brochure has pictures or graphics that go well with the information.

☐ I checked the spelling.

☐ I checked the punctuation.

☐ My brochure is attractive.

Energy Vocabulary

1. In each group of words below, circle the one that does not belong. On the line below the group of words, explain why the word does not belong.

   a) reduce   dump   reuse   recycle

   _____

   b) coal   natural gas   biomass   oil

   _____

   c) kinetic   chemical   harvested   gravitational

   _____

   d) geothermal   hydroelectricity   solar   fossil fuels

   _____

2. Unscramble the letters to make energy words.

   a) n b w e e l r e a   _____

   b) r c t x a e e d t   _____

   c) s r v c o i o n n e a t   _____

   d) t o e m p e u l r   _____

   e) f n a o r r t o n t s m i a   _____

3. Write a definition for each of the unscrambled words from question 2.

   a) _____

   _____

   b) _____

   _____

   c) _____

   _____

   d) _____

   _____

   e) _____

   _____

Conserving Energy

We use energy every day. We use it to make our lives comfortable and enjoyable. But we must remember that the supply of energy is not limitless. To keep our way of life, we need to use our energy resources wisely. By saving energy ourselves, we can also help others in the world have a good life. Conserving will also make sure people in the future have energy for their needs.

New Technologies

Many new technologies have been developed that can help us save energy. Here are some examples:

- Electric and hybrid cars: These cars use less gasoline. They help reduce the amount of oil used.
- Plants as plastic: Plastic products can be made from plant materials. This will conserve oil, since most plastic is made from oil.
- Solar power plants to generate electricity: Solar energy will always be available. It is Earth's most available energy source. Using solar energy will conserve other energy sources.
- Compact fluorescent light bulbs: These bulbs produce the same amount of light as incandescent bulbs, but they use less energy. So using compact fluorescent bulbs saves electricity.

In the Home

Appliances such as stoves are the main source of energy use in homes. Other examples are washers, furnaces, and water heaters. Two programs help people buy appliances and equipment that use less electricity.

- EnerGuide: This is a Canadian government requirement. All appliances and equipment must have a label that shows the amount of energy they use.
- Energy Star®: This is an international program. This label is put on appliances and equipment that are the most energy efficient.

You Are Important

You can do many things to conserve energy. Think about all the things you do at home, at school, and everywhere else. How do you use energy? How could you reduce the energy you use? What help do you need from others to reduce energy use?

"Conserving Energy"—Think About It!

1. Write a persuasive paragraph on why it is important to save energy. Use information from the text and your own ideas.

_____

_____

_____

_____

_____

_____

_____

_____

_____

_____

_____

_____

_____

_____

_____

_____

_____

_____

_____

_____

_____

_____

_____

2. Which type of energy do you think is more important to save: energy that comes from natural gas, or from hydroelectricity? Why?

_____

_____

_____

3. Solar energy technology is very expensive to build. This is one reason why it is not widely used yet. What might be another reason why it is not widely used?

_____

_____

_____

4. You can help conserve energy. Below are some objects you might use or activities you might do. For each one, tell how you could use the object or do the activity to save energy. The first one is done for you.

   a) Refrigerator: Do not stand with the door open while thinking about what you want to eat.

   b) Lights in a bedroom:_____

   c) Hair dryer: _____

   d) Brushing teeth: _____

   e) Washing clothes: _____

   f) Taking a bath: _____

   g) Television: _____

   h) Computer: _____

   i) Dishwasher: _____

   j) Going to school: _____

Share your ideas with a classmate.

The Impact of Resource and Energy Use

It is important to conserve natural resources so they will available for future use. But there are other things to think about when it comes to resource and energy use. Resource and energy use can have an impact on people and the environment in many ways.

Harvesting or Extracting Natural Resources

The harvesting or extracting of natural resources can have an impact. For example, open-pit mines are used to mine many types of minerals. This means that huge holes are dug in the land to find the minerals. These mines can pollute rivers and streams. They can also add to air pollution.

mining

Logging forests (cutting down the trees) can also have impacts. Habitats for plants and animals can be destroyed. When trees are cut, soil can be washed away by heavy rain and blown away by wind.

Resources are turned into useful items in processing plants. These plants can also add to air and water pollution. They also use very large amounts of energy.

Today in Canada, people are very concerned about damaging the environment. All levels of government have laws to protect the environment. These laws make sure companies lessen their impact on the environment. Companies often develop new procedures to help in this effort.

Consultation

How are decisions made about resource production? For example, what happens when a company wants to open a mine? One of the most important things that happens is consultation. This means that people get together to give their opinions and ideas about the project. These people may include scientists, environmentalists, politicians, people from the company, and people from the community. Sometimes these consultations can go on for years before a decision is made.

The final decision is made by either the provincial or federal government, or both. To make the decision, the government considers the benefits of the project, as well as the concerns. The resource produced by a mine might be in great demand. If the resource is in demand, the economy of the community will improve. This could mean more jobs for people in the community. It could also mean more money for things such as schools and hospitals.

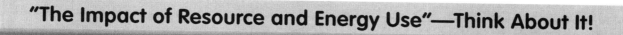

Everyone Has an Opinion

A large electric company wants to build a dam and a hydroelectric power plant to generate electricity. On the negative side, building the dam and plant will change the environment. They will have to move lots of earth and build roads. A huge amount of land behind the dam will be flooded to create a reservoir. The normal flow of the river will be stopped. This would affect the plants and fish in the river. Tourists visit the area because it has beautiful scenery. They also like to fish in the river. If the dam is built, tourism will probably be affected.

On the positive side, the power plant will produce clean and inexpensive power. This power can be sold to bring money into the community. Right now, there are only a few tourism jobs for people in the town near the river. Many people have moved away. Building the dam will mean lots of jobs.

1. Think about the following people and the opinions they might have. Decide whether each one would support or oppose the dam. Give reasons for your ideas.

a) People from the town who need jobs: _____

_____

_____

b) Scientists who are concerned about the impact on the environment: _____

_____

_____

c) The local town government: _____

_____

_____

d) People from nearby communities who want cheaper electricity: _____

_____

_____

e) People who fish in the river:_____

_____

_____

Take One Point of View

Read the statement. It is important for government to consult many different people on projects such as building a dam and a hydroelectric power plant to generate electricity.

1. Do you agree or disagree with this statement? Use the outline below to plan your writing.

A Statement of Your Point of View	
Main Idea	**Supporting Evidence**
Main Idea	**Supporting Evidence**
Main Idea	**Supporting Evidence**

STEM-Related Occupations

To learn more about some of these occupations visit the following websites:

http://www.sciencebuddies.org/science-engineering-careers

https://kids.usa.gov/watch-videos/index.shtml

Accountant
Aerospace Engineer
Agricultural Engineer
Agricultural Technician
Aircraft Mechanic and
    Service Technician
Animal Breeder
Animal Trainer
Animator
Anthropologist
Architect
Astronaut
Astronomer
Athletic Trainer
Audio Engineer
Audiologist
Automotive Mechanic
Biochemical Engineer
Biochemist/Biophysicist
Biologist
Biology Teacher
Biomedical Engineer
Business Owner
Cardiovascular Technician
Carpenter
Chef
Chemical Engineer
Chemical Technician
Chemistry Teacher
Chiropractor
Civil Engineer
Civil Engineering Technician
Climate Change Analyst
Clinical Psychologist
Computer Engineer
Computer Programmer
Computer Systems Analyst
Construction Manager
Counselling Psychologist
Dietetic Technician

Dietitian and Nutritionist
Doctor
Electrical Engineering Technician
Electrician
Electronics Engineer
Emergency Medical Technician
Environmental Engineer
Environmental Engineering Technician
Environmental Restoration Planner
Environmental Scientist
Epidemiologist
Fire-Prevention Engineer
Fish and Game Worker
Food Science Technician
Food Scientist and Technologist
Forest and Conservation Technician
Forest and Conservation Worker
Geoscientist
Graphic Designer
Hydrologist
Industrial Engineer
Interior Designer
Landscape Architect
Manufacturing Engineer
Marine Architect
Marine Biologist
Math Teacher
Mechanical Engineer
Mechanical Engineering Technician
Medical Lab Technician
Medical Scientist
Meteorologist
Microbiologist
Microsystems Engineer
Mining and Geological Engineer
Molecular and Cellular Biologist
Neurologist
Nuclear Engineer
Nursery and Greenhouse Manager
Nutritionist

Occupational Health and Safety Specialist
Optical Engineer
Optometrist
Paleontologist
Patent Lawyer
Pathologist
Park Ranger
Petroleum Engineer
Pharmacist
Physical Therapist
Physician
Physician Assistant
Physicist
Pilot
Psychologist
Registered Nurse
Respiratory Therapist
Robotics Engineer
Robotics Technician
School Psychologist
Seismologist
Software Developer (Applications)
Software Developer (Systems Software)
Soil and Plant Scientist
Soil and Water Conservationist
Space Scientist
Speech-Language Pathologist
Statistician
Transportation Engineer
Transportation Planner
Urban Planner
Veterinarian
Video Game Designer
Volcanologist
Water/Wastewater Engineer
Wind Energy Engineer
X-ray Technician
Zookeeper
Zoologist
Wildlife Biologist

Science, Technology, Engineering, and Mathematics (STEM) Occupation Brochure

Create a brochure about a STEM-related occupation.

STEP 1: Plan Your Brochure

❑ Take a piece of paper and fold the paper the same way your brochure will be folded. Before writing the brochure, plan the layout in pencil. Sections of the brochure should include
- Job description
- Training or degree needed
- Work environment
- How the occupation relates to STEM
- Interesting facts

❑ Write the heading for each section where you would like it to be in the brochure.

❑ Plan where graphics or pictures will be placed in the brochure.

STEP 2: Complete a Draft

❑ Research information for each section of your brochure. Check your facts.

❑ Read your draft for meaning, then add, delete, or change words to make your writing better.

❑ Plan what illustrations or graphics you will put into your brochure.

STEP 3: Checklist

❑ My brochure is neat and well organized.

❑ My brochure has accurate information.

❑ My brochure has pictures or graphics that go well with the information.

❑ I checked the spelling.

❑ I checked the punctuation.

❑ My brochure is attractive.

What Does a Marine Biologist Do?

Marine Biologists

Biologists study living things, including plants and animals. A marine biologist is someone who studies plants and animals that live in the ocean. Thousands of different plants and animals live in the ocean, so many marine biologists choose to study just one thing. For example, a marine biologist might decide to study dolphins, sharks, or seaweed.

Where Marine Biologists Do Their Work

Some marine biologists work on a boat. They might watch whales that come to the ocean's surface and observe how they behave and where they travel. Marine biologists might also use underwater cameras to watch animals that do not come to the surface.

Other marine biologists go down into the ocean. Some are scuba divers who collect underwater plants so they can learn more about them. The scuba divers might also collect marine animals. They study the animals to learn about how their bodies work and whether they have any diseases.

Sometimes marine biologists use a small type of submarine to go into the ocean. The submarine has bright lights and lots of clear plastic so people can see what is happening under the ocean's surface.

Some marine biologists work in laboratories, observing fish in large water tanks, or looking at tiny sea creatures under a microscope.

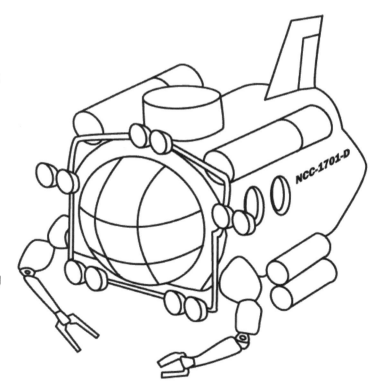

Becoming a Marine Biologist

If you are interested in becoming a marine biologist, learn to read and write well. Marine biologists read and write many scientific reports. You should also work hard at science. People take lots of science courses at university to become marine biologists.

This small submarine has lots of lights for seeing things in deep water, and claws for picking things up off the ocean floor.

"What Does a Marine Biologist Do?"—Think About It!

1. Write a definition for marine animals.

_____

_____

2. Different types of scientists often become experts in one particular topic. Is this true of marine biologists? Give evidence from the article to support your answer.

_____

_____

_____

3. Some marine biologists do not go down into the ocean. What are three examples of ways these marine biologists study ocean animals?

_____

_____

_____

4. Scuba divers and small submarines cannot stay underwater for very long periods of time. Why?

_____

_____

_____

5. The illustration shows a small submarine that marine biologists might use. Write two things you learned about this submarine from the illustration.

_____

_____

_____

6. What is one way that marine biologists share the information they learn?

_____

_____

What Does a Carpenter Do?

A carpenter uses tools to join together pieces of wood to build structures.

Getting Started

Battery powered drill

Before carpenters can start building, they need to have a plan to follow. The plan is a diagram of the structure they are going to build. The diagram gives all the measurements of the structure. Carpenters use the plan to figure out how much wood they will need, what size and shape each piece of wood needs to be, and what tools will be needed.

Building with Tools

Carpenters use power tools and hand tools. Power tools get their power from electricity. Examples of power tools are electric saws, drills, and sanders. Hand tools do not use electricity. Carpenters use their muscles for power when they use hand tools such as hammers and hand saws.

Types of Carpenters

Handsaw

Carpenters are divided into different categories, depending on the type of work they do. Construction carpenters work on building large structures, such as new homes, office buildings, and stores. Residential carpenters work on homes that have already been built. They might put new wood floors in a house, repair the roof, or add a deck to the back of the house. Furniture makers build different types of wooden furniture. For example, if you want new kitchen cupboards, a bookshelf, or a table, a furniture maker can make what you need in the exact size and shape that you want.

Skills

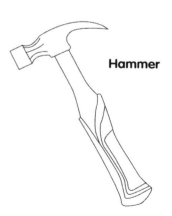
Hammer

Here are some examples of skills that carpenters need:
- Math skills: Carpenters use math skills when they add, subtract, multiply, or divide different measurements.
- Safety skills: Carpenters need to know how to use tools safely.
- Drawing skills: When furniture makers design a new piece of furniture, they make a drawing to show the customer what it will look like.

1. All carpenters use nails, screws, and glue to make things. Why are these materials important in any carpenter's job?

_____

_____

2. The article mentions electric saws, drills, and sanders. Why did the author provide these examples of tools?

_____

_____

3. Power tools need electricity to work. Hand tools also need a source of energy to do work. Where does this energy come from?

_____

_____

4. Which kind of carpenter would you need for each of the projects below?

Building a bridge: _____

Replacing a home's old staircase: _____

5. The word *residential* comes from the word *residence*. Use information from the article to help you write a definition of residence.

_____

_____

6. How is putting together a wooden bookshelf from a store similar to and different from a furniture maker's job?

Similar: _____

_____

Different: _____

_____

What Does an Engineer Do?

Engineers are people who build all types of things that make our world work better. Many of the things you see and use every day were created by engineers. Some engineers work with chemicals to create new textiles, more flexible plastics, and stronger building materials. Others work in cities to build roads, bridges, and skyscrapers. Some engineers make medical supplies for hospitals, technology for space travel, and find new and safer ways to clean up the environment. Engineers can build or create just about anything!

There are many different types of engineers.

Civil engineers make structures and systems that help cities and industries work and grow. They build bridges, highways, railways, skyscrapers, engines and machines, airplanes and rocket ships.

Chemical engineers work with chemicals to find new ways of producing and improving the goods we use. They make such things as safer foods, softer and warmer clothing, new types of plastics, and textiles that do not catch fire.

Environmental engineers work to find ways of solving problems that affect animals, plants, and humans. They find ways to clean up polluted water and air, and to safely dispose of toxic wastes to make Earth cleaner and safer.

Audio engineers work with sound, and the programs and equipment that create, record, and share that sound. They create the music, audio books, and radio programs we listen to. They also create the fun and exciting sound effects and music for movies, television shows, and video games.

Computer engineers create programs to run your computer and to make it more useful and fun. They also help provide hospitals with programs that control X-ray machines and keep track of patient information.

Optical engineers make technologies that use and control light. These engineers create eyeglasses, camera lenses, televisions, telescopes, microscopes, lasers, solar cells, and broadband networks that bring the Internet into homes.

Electrical engineers work with electricity. They help build power stations. They also design the power lines that carry the electricity to where it is needed. Electricity helps your furnace to heat your home, and powers your lights, phone, computer, television, and appliances. Electricity also powers streetlights, traffic lights, and entire cities.

Can you imagine what life would be like without paved roads, radios, computers, phones, television, refrigerators, plastics, apartment buildings, or electric lights? Without the hard work of so many types of engineers, our lives would be very different!

1. What type of engineer would you like to be? Explain why.

_____

_____

_____

_____

_____

_____

2. How do engineers help people in their daily life?

_____

_____

_____

_____

_____

_____

_____

Satellites in Space

A satellite is any object that circles, or orbits, a planet or another natural object in space. The Moon is Earth's only natural satellite. But zooming around our planet are thousands of artificial (human-made) satellites. Life on Earth would be very different without them.

What Satellites Do

Today there are about 3000 artificial satellites orbiting Earth. Why have companies and countries put so many into space? Some satellites transmit voice, data, and video communications from one location on Earth to another. For example, many people use a service called satellite TV at home. The television station sends the television signal to a satellite. The satellite then sends the signal to a satellite dish at your home.

Other satellites provide a way for people to communicate with ships and planes. There are also scientific research satellites, which gather and send information to Earth, including information about weather.

Many drivers use a Global Positioning System (GPS) device to get directions to their destinations. The GPS relies on more than 20 satellites to figure out a user's exact location.

The Parts of a Satellite

The diagram below shows some of the main parts of a satellite.

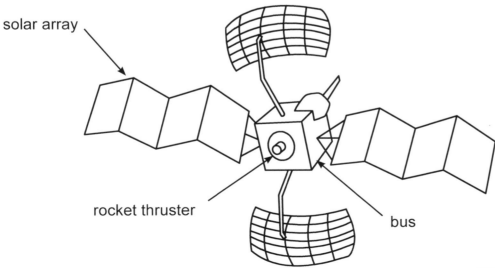

solar array

rocket thruster

bus

continued next page

What Do the Various Parts of a Satellite Do?

- Antennas receive radio signals from Earth. A satellite also has transmitters, which send signals to Earth.
- Solar arrays turn sunlight into electricity to power the satellite. The arrays can turn so they continue to face the Sun as the satellite moves in its orbit.
- Rechargeable batteries in the bus store electricity from the solar arrays.
- Rocket thrusters can be turned on to overcome the pull of gravity and keep the satellite in its orbit. Gravity from Earth or the Moon could pull a satellite out of its orbit.
- Fuel tanks inside the bus provide fuel for the thrusters.
- Computers in the bus tell the satellite what to do. Scientists on Earth can control the computers and provide new instructions when they want the satellite to do something different.
- Cameras and telescopes are attached to the bus on some satellites. These devices capture visual information, such as pictures of a planet.

Most of the equipment on satellites is very sensitive, and it needs to be protected from very hot and very cold temperatures. The side of a satellite that faces the Sun can become extremely hot, while the side that does not receive sunlight gets very cold. Layered blankets that look like aluminum foil on the outside can be used to keep heat in. Electrical equipment can be kept cool through the use of radiators, which release heat.

Collisions in Space

Because there are so many satellites circling Earth, with more being launched all the time, the chance that two will collide is increasing. In 2009, it actually happened—an American communications satellite was destroyed when a dead Russian satellite crashed into it.

The International Space Station

The International Space Station (ISS) is our planet's most famous artificial satellite. But Earth is not the only planet with human-made satellites. There are space probes orbiting Mars, Mercury, Jupiter, Saturn, and Venus. There are also artificial satellites circling the Sun, Moon, and asteroids. These satellites send back information that helps scientists learn more about the solar system.

What Do Aerospace and Satellite Engineers Do?

Aerospace engineers design satellites, spacecraft, and airplanes. Satellite engineers create computer programs that give instructions to orbiting satellites and keep them functioning properly.

"Satellites in Space"—Think About It

1. The introductory paragraph says that life on Earth would be very different without artificial satellites. Provide two examples from the article of how the lives of average people (not scientists) would be different.

_____

_____

_____

_____

_____

2. As a satellite orbits Earth, there are times when Earth is between the Sun and the satellite, so sunlight cannot reach the satellite's solar arrays. How does the satellite get electricity to keep working when no sunlight is reaching the solar arrays?

_____

_____

_____

_____

_____

3. Does the International Space Station orbit Earth, or does it travel among the planets in our solar system? Use information from the article to support your answer.

_____

_____

_____

_____

_____

Think Like an Engineer!

An engineer is a person who designs and build things. Engineers want to understand how and why things work. Engineers try different ideas, learn from their mistakes, then try again. Engineers call these steps the design process.

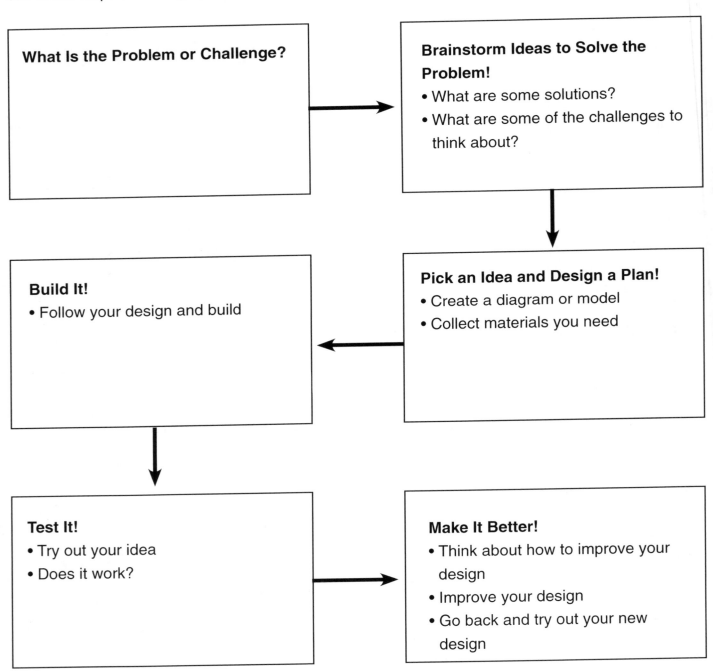

What Is the Problem or Challenge?

Brainstorm Ideas to Solve the Problem!
- What are some solutions?
- What are some of the challenges to think about?

Build It!
- Follow your design and build

Pick an Idea and Design a Plan!
- Create a diagram or model
- Collect materials you need

Test It!
- Try out your idea
- Does it work?

Make It Better!
- Think about how to improve your design
- Improve your design
- Go back and try out your new design

Remember to be patient. Take your time to figure things out.

The Design Process

1. What is the problem or challenge?

_____

_____

_____

2. Brainstorm! What are some solutions? List any possible challenges to think about.

_____

_____

_____

_____

_____

_____

_____

_____

_____

continued next page ☞

3. Pick a design idea! Draw and label a diagram of your design. Add notes about your design plan.

continued next page ☞

4. Get ready! What materials do you need? Collect the materials you will need.

_____

_____

_____

_____

_____

_____

Other notes:

_____

_____

_____

_____

_____

_____

_____

continued next page 👉

5. Test it! Build your design and try it out.

Did it work? Yes ☐ A little ☐ No ☐

6. Make it better! How can you make your design better?

_____

_____

_____

7. Go back! Try your design out again. What happened?

_____

_____

_____

8. What do you wonder about?

_____

_____

_____

9. What are you proud of?

_____

_____

Inventor Oral Presentation Outline

Choose an invention you are interested in. Research the inventor and how the invention was created. Think about how the invention has helped people or changed the world. Some ideas include

- a type of medicine such as penicillin
- transportation such as a car or an airplane
- an everyday item such as a zipper or camera

Inventor: _____

Invention: _____

Introduction Checklist

I introduced my topic in an attention-grabbing way, such as

❏ a quote

❏ a statistic

❏ an example

❏ a question

❏ I state what I am going to talk about in 1 to 3 sentences.

_____

_____

_____

_____

_____

continued next page ☞

Body Checklist

❑ My main point has supporting details, examples, or descriptions.

❑ I wrote out my ideas the way I would sound if I were explaining, showing, or telling someone in person during a conversation.

❑ I read aloud what I wrote.

Tip: You do not have to use full sentences. Write it the same way you talk.

Main Point

_____

_____

_____

Supporting Details

_____

_____

_____

_____

_____

_____

_____

_____

_____

_____

continued next page ☞

Conclusion Checklist

❑ I summarized my key points.

❑ I ended my oral presentation in an attention-grabbing way, such as

❑ a quote

❑ a statistic

❑ a question

_____

_____

_____

_____

_____

_____

_____

_____

_____

_____

Presentation Delivery Tips

- Practice! Practice! Practice! Get comfortable with what you have written.
- Highlight your good copy in places where you would like to pause for effect, or emphasize a point.
- Think about hand gestures and making eye contact with the audience or camera.
- Think about your tone of voice to show enthusiasm, emotion, or volume.

STEM Rubric

	Level 1 Below Expectations	Level 2 Approaches Expectations	Level 3 Meets Expectations	Level 4 Exceeds Expectations
Knowledge of STEM Concepts	• Displays little understanding of concepts. • Rarely gives complete explanations. • Intensive teacher support is needed.	• Displays a satisfactory understanding of most concepts. • Sometimes gives appropriate, but incomplete explanations. • Teacher support is sometimes needed.	• Displays a considerable understanding of most concepts. • Usually gives complete or nearly complete explanations. • Infrequent teacher support is needed.	• Displays a thorough understanding of all or almost all concepts. • Consistently gives appropriate and complete explanations independently. • No teacher support is needed.
Application of STEM Concepts	• Relates STEM concepts to outside world with extensive teacher prompts. • Application of concepts rarely appropriate and accurate.	• Relates STEM concepts to outside world with some teacher prompts. • Application of concepts sometimes appropriate and accurate.	• Relates STEM concepts to outside world with few teacher prompts. • Application of concepts usually appropriate and accurate.	• Relates STEM concepts to outside world independently. • Application of concepts almost always appropriate and accurate.
Written Communication of Ideas	• Expresses ideas with limited critical thinking skills. • Few ideas are well organized and effective.	• Expresses ideas with some critical thinking skills. • Some ideas are well organized and effective.	• Expresses ideas with considerable critical thinking skills. • Most ideas are well organized and effective.	• Expresses ideas with in-depth critical thinking skills. • Ideas are well organized and effective.
Oral Communication of Ideas	• Rarely uses correct STEM terminology when discussing STEM concepts.	• Sometimes uses correct STEM terminology when discussing STEM concepts.	• Usually uses correct STEM terminology when discussing STEM concepts.	• Consistently uses correct STEM terminology when discussing STEM concepts.

Notes: _____

_____

_____

STEM Focus _____

Student's Name	Knowledge of STEM Concepts	Application of STEM Concepts	Written Communication of Ideas	Oral Communication Skills	Overall Mark

STEM Expert!

Incredible work!

Great Work!

Keep up the effort!

Unit: Human Body Systems

Your Respiratory System, pages 2–4

1. a) nose and mouth
   b) nasal cavity
   c) pharynx
   d) larynx
   e) trachea
   f) bronchioles
   g) alveoli

2. When you have a cold, your nose and throat are more sensitive and congested. That makes you sneeze, cough, and develop a sore throat. Your nose tries to keep germs out of your throat. To do this, it makes more mucus than usual and that is why your nose runs.

Experiment: How Much Air? page 5

1. Answers will vary.

2. In step 3, the air breathed into the bottle pushes water out of the bottle. The volume of the air that went into the bottle is equal to the volume of water pushed out. It also takes the same volume of water to refill the bottle.

Your Circulatory System, pages 6–7

1. a) Answers will vary.
   b) Answers will vary.
   c) The active pulse should be a higher number.

2. a) The neck pulse is stronger than the wrist pulse.
   b) Students should feel the neck pulse first.
   c) The artery in your neck is larger than the one in your wrist. This is one reason the pulse is stronger. Also, your neck is closer to your heart than your wrist is. That makes the pulse in your neck stronger. That also means you feel it slightly sooner than you feel it in your wrist. The blood gets to your neck faster than it gets to your wrist.

Your Digestive System, pages 8–9

1. a) mouth
   b) esophagus
   c) stomach
   d) small intestine
   e) large intestine
   f) rectum

2. esophagus, small intestine, large intestine, and rectum

3. Sample answers: teeth—candy corn; esophagus—toilet paper tube; stomach—baggie; small intestine—ramen noodles; large intestine—hose; liver, pancreas, and gall bladder—modelling clay or rubber foam

4. a) The front teeth because they are sharpest.
   b) The side and back teeth because they are flat and can grind food between them.

Your Bones and Skeleton, page 10

Sample answers:

1. a) elbow; b) hip; c) neck

2. The bones in my legs support my hips and upper body.

3. The skull protects the brain.

4. Bones support your body and joints help the parts bend.

The Muscles of Your Body, pages 11–12

1. a) Sample answers: athlete; boxer; construction worker; delivery person; dog walker; farmer; firefighter; lifeguard; soldier; personal trainer
   b) Sample answers: sitting up straight; walking from place to place; reaching for objects; typing; moving a computer mouse

3. diaphragm

4. Muscle on front of arm (biceps).

5. Muscle on back of arm (triceps).

6. heart

Your Nervous System, pages 13–15

1. Descriptions should include the nerves reacting, observing, making motion, and maintaining the body (e.g., breathing and heart beating).

Experiment 1: Students should catch the ruler more quickly as they become more familiar with the experiment. In dim light, reflexes will likely be slower. Students cannot see the ruler as well in dim light.

Experiment 2: Results will vary.

Experiment 3: Crossing your fingers confuses your brain. Your brain does not usually receive these type of signals from your fingers. You make your brain think you must be feeling two separate things.

Overview of the Human _____ System, page 16

Ensure that students' answers relate to the body system they have chosen.

Sunlight and Vitamin D, pages 17–18

Sample answers:

1. wear sunscreen; cover your skin; limit time in sunlight; stay indoors during hottest time of day

2. exercise outside; meet with friends for an outdoor activity; read outside; help with outside chores; eat a meal outside; go for walks

3. Advantages—get vitamin D your body needs for strong bones and disease prevention; you are outside breathing fresh air; you are likely moving and getting exercise; sunshine makes most people feel happier
   Disadvantages—sunburn damages your skin (may lead to cancer); overheating; dehydration

Healthy Eating: Journal Topics, page 19

Look for evidence that students are using the information they learned to make reasoned arguments.

Fitness and Health, pages 20–21

1. Sample answer: Eat nutritious food; drink a lot of water; exercise daily; get enough sleep; wear protective equipment; do not smoke; use sunscreen; get enough sunlight

2. Sample answer: more energy, healthier body, healthier heart, breathing easier, stronger muscles, fun

Create a Human Body Board Game, page 22
Encourage students to test their board games with a partner to receive feedback.

Unit: Forces Acting on Structures and Mechanisms

Two Basic Forces: Pushing and Pulling, pages 23–24
1. a) You push the mouse from side to side to move the cursor back and forth. You push the mouse away from you to move the cursor up. You pull the mouse toward you to move the cursor down.
   b) You push and pull on the toothbrush to move it back and forth across your teeth. You push the brush against your teeth to apply light pressure.
   c) You push down on the pedals to move forward. To turn, you push the handlebars with one hand and pull with the other. To stop, you pull or squeeze the brake levers. To change gears, you push or pull the gear shifters.
2. Sample answer: In volleyball, you push the ball to serve. You also push the ball to send it back over the net during play. Gravity pulls the ball toward the ground.
3. Shape: The pushing force causes a change in the shape of the balloon by forcing it to become larger and more rounded.

Forces and Structures, pages 25–26
1. a) dead load; pipes do not move and never leave
   b) dead load; the elevator is permanently attached; the passengers are a live load
   c) live load; workers move and can leave
   d) live load; wind does not blow all the time
   e) dead load; balconies are permanently attached to the structure

Four Types of Internal Forces, pages 27–28
1. Compression; the weight of Ling's body pushes down on the mattress, squeezing it. The height of the mattress (when horizontal) becomes thinner.
2. a) Tension is acting on the strings. The tuning pegs pull on the strings. The strings stretch when Rick tightens them.
   b) Rick turns the tuning pegs. Torsion is acting on the pegs. Torsion is a twisting or turning force.
3. Bending acts on the wire. Maria and Marco must bend the wire to make it into a circular shape. Bending involves compression and tension.
4. Tension acts on the fishing line because it is being pulled from both ends. Mr. Green pulls on one end as he reels in the line. The fish pulls on the other end as it tries to swim away.

Experimenting with Materials and Forces, pages 29–30
Answers will vary as the rating scale is subjective. You might ask students to compare their results for different items or with a classmate.

Forces and Shapes, pages 31–32
1. compression
2. a) compression
   b) tension
3. a) The weight of the snow will push down on the roof, possibly causing it to bend or collapse.
   b) A triangular roof would be safer. The sloped sides of the roof make it easier for snow to slide off. (Gravity will pull it down to the ground.) Snow will not slide off a flat roof. The weight of snow might cause a flat roof to collapse.
   c) Rain will quickly run off the roof.
4. a) a dome and an arch
   b) Create buttresses of snow against the two sides of the arch.

Four Types of Bridges, pages 33–34
1. External, because they are temporary.
2. a) Compression acts on the blocks. The weight of the person on the bridge is transferred through the plank to the blocks. It pushes down on the blocks.
   b) Bending, or compression on the top of the plank and tension on the bottom.
   c) Internal, because it is part of the structure.
3. a) It tells you how much weight the bridge will have to support for each bus.
   b) It tells you the maximum weight the bridge may have to support.

Plastic Straw Bridge Challenge, page 35
Designs will vary. Look for evidence that students considered the strength of shapes and style of bridges.

The Incredible Chunnel, pages 36–38
1. If two TBMs work on the same tunnel, the tunnel can be completed twice as quickly.
2. The Chunnel designers would need to create a way for a train to turn around so it could make the journey back to the other side of the Chunnel.
3. Answers will vary. Students should provide at least one reason to support their response.

Watch Out for Wind! pages 39–40
1. Sample answers: Most basements are built below the ground. So the force of the wind will not push on the basement walls. There is little danger that wind will cause basement walls to collapse.
2. The blanket helps protect you from flying glass and other debris.
3. The pointed rings of the nails will grab onto the surrounding wood. This helps to prevent the nail from being pulled out of the boards.
4. The rounded shape of a dome home allows wind to flow around and over it. So less force would push on a dome than would push on a house with straight walls.

Earthquake! pages 41–43
Sample answers:
1. The base of the seismometer moves back and forth as the ground shakes. The paper is sitting on the base, so the paper moves with the base. A zigzag line is drawn because the paper is moving back and forth, not the weight.
2. Vibrations from the train travel through the ground as waves of energy. These waves travel from the ground into my body, so I feel the vibrations.
3. Seismologists study waves that travel through the ground. A volcano that is about to erupt might send waves through the ground, and seismologists could use seismometers to detect these waves.

Protect Yourself! pages 44–45
1. Goalies block shots with their legs. The thick pads protect the goalie's legs from the force of a fast-moving puck.
2. a) When you run, your feet hit the ground with greater force than when you walk. The impact or shock can cause injury. Cushioned soles help to absorb some of the impact.
   b) Compression is created when body weight pushes the shoe against the ground. The soles bend because the back of the shoe is lifted off the ground before the front. Soles that do not hold up under these forces will crack and break.
3. In a tight helmet, your head is already causing compression on the foam. The compressed foam then provides less protection to the wearer. Because of this, it cannot absorb as much compression from outside forces.
4. Gravity makes objects speed up as they approach Earth. So a skateboarder who is standing will hit the ground with a lot of force. But a skateboarder who is low to the ground will hit the ground with less force. This skateboarder will likely have less serious injuries than they would if they were standing.

Structures and the Environment, pages 46–47
1. Sample answers: damages the area that the materials are taken from; transporting and processing materials makes pollution, the construction process damages the area around them.
2. Sample answers: The ferry's engine will burn gasoline, which causes air pollution. Gasoline and oil from the ferry could leak into the river. This would affect plants and fish. The noise of the ferry's engine and propeller could affect fish and plant populations.
3. a) They would likely want a bridge because it could provide them with construction jobs.
   b) They would likely want the bridge because a ferry would disturb the fish and could damage the habitat.

Forces and Structures Quiz, page 48
1. speed, direction, shape
2. The pulling force of gravity makes the ball slow down as it travels upward. Eventually, the ball will change direction and gravity will pull it back to Earth. The ball will travel faster as it

gets closer to Earth.
3. External forces come from things that are not part of the structure. Internal forces act within the structure.
4. a) torsion
   b) bending
   c) tension
   d) compression
5. Sample answer: triangle, dome
6. Answers will vary.

Unit: Properties of and Changes in Matter

What Is Matter? pages 49–50
1. All examples are made of matter.
2. a) B
   b) The two objects might not contain the same number of particles (or amount of matter).
3. a) a watermelon
   b) a quarter
4. a) volume
   b) greater (more) volume

Properties of Matter, pages 51–52
1. Sample answers: It is soft so it does not scratch skin or dishes; it can easily change shape to make drying a person or dish easier; and it does not dissolve in water.
2. a) a high viscosity
   b) Sample answer: red, sweet, cold, liquid
3. It allows you to see the food through the wrap.
4. a) The powder did not dissolve well and most of it settled to the bottom of the glass.
5. Sample answer: hard, writing height, brown, metal

Experiment: Do All Liquids Dissolve in Water? pages 53–54
1–6. Observations may vary. The alcohol and corn syrup should appear to dissolve. But the vegetable oil will not dissolve. It will float on top of the water.
7. No, not all liquids dissolve in water.

States of Matter, pages 55–56
1. Solid—a pencil, an elastic band
   Liquid—a drop of water, ink in a marker, flowing lava
   Gas—oxygen in the air, steam from hot soup
2. a) False
   b) False
   c) False
   d) The substance must be a gas because it does not have a definite volume. It can also expand to take up more space without changing state. Solids and liquids cannot do this.
3. a) a gas
   b) The gas has spread out to fill its container (the elevator). So the scent (which is a property of the gas) is the same strength throughout the elevator.

Experiment: What State Is It In? pages 57–58
Explanatory note: Shaving foam is made of liquid soap. It has many gas bubbles mixed into it. The gas adds stiffness to the liquid soap. It also helps the foam keep its shape. This is why it can support the nickel. After being exposed to the air for two or three days, the gas escapes into the air and leaves behind solid soap. It also leaves tiny spaces where the gas bubbles were. Fresh shaving foam is a liquid combined with a gas. The shaving foam left in the open for two or three days is a solid.

Changes in States of Matter, pages 59–61
1. a) gas, liquid
   b) solid, melting
   c) gas
   d) deposition
   e) evaporation
   f) liquid, solid
   g) absorbed
   h) absorbed
   i) released
   j) absorbed
   k) released
   l) released
2. a) evaporation
   b) deposition
   c) freezing

Physical Changes and Chemical Changes, pages 62–63
1. Physical changes—Molten lava hardening into rock; Cracking open an egg; Crumpling tin foil; Breaking a glass. Chemical changes—Baking cookie dough; Bread becoming mouldy; Cooking rice; Lighting a match; Digesting food; Toasting bread

Experiment: Observing a Chemical Change, pages 64–65
1. Pictures should show a flat balloon on the left and a very inflated balloon on the right.
2. Bubbles form in the liquid and the balloon inflates.
3. The balloon is going through a physical change because the change can be reversed—the balloon can be deflated.

Breakfast Science, page 66
Sample answer:
Orange Juice—melting and mixing (p)
Scrambled eggs—cracking and mixing (p), frying (c)
Toast—toasting (c), slicing (p)
Bacon—frying (c)
Pancakes—mixing (p), frying (c)
Oatmeal—heating in water (p)

What Is So Great About Gases? pages 67–68
1. A gas will spread out to fill its container (the air bag).
2. The solid air freshener changes state to become a gas. It gives off a scent and the scent spreads out to fill the room. This is because a gas spreads out to fill its container. The air freshener changes from a solid into a gas without first

becoming a liquid (melting). So the air freshener goes through the process of sublimation.

Brain Stretch, page 68
The material the balloon is made from contains microscopic holes. The particles of helium gas escape through these holes over time. (Helium balloons are often made from a foil material. That is because foil contains fewer microscopic holes than latex does. A foil balloon will deflate more slowly than a latex balloon.)

Changes of State Review, page 69
1. melting, absorbed
2. evaporation, absorbed
3. deposition, released
4. freezing (or solidification), released
5. condensation, released
6. sublimation, absorbed

Matter Word Search, page 70
1. solid
2. volume
3. physical
4. solubility
5. gas
6. mass
7. viscosity
8. chemical

Unit: Conservation of Energy and Resources

Natural Resources, pages 71–72
1. Sample answer: Living Things—leaves, birds, frogs, snails, grass
   Non-living Things—soil, volcanoes, gold, aluminum, mountains
2. a) renewable
   b) non-renewable
   c) renewable
   d) non-renewable
   e) renewable
   f) renewable

g) non-renewable

h) renewable

3. a) Glass bottles are a renewable product. Sand is always being formed through the erosion of rock. So sand is a renewable resource.

b) Plastic bottles are a non-renewable product. They are made from oil, which is a non-renewable resource.

Using Resources, pages 73–74

1. The products do not look like the resources they are made from.

2. Sample answers:

a) Any fish or seafood, any plants, any animals

b) Any minerals, coal, natural gas

3. Copper ore contains copper, but it also contains other things. Copper used to make pipes is pure copper.

4. Step should be in the following order:

1) Trees are cut down.

2) Bark is rubbed off the trees.

3) Logs are cut into chips.

4) Chips are cooked with chemicals to make pulp.

5) Pulp is bleached to make it white.

6) Pulp is dried and pressed to make paper.

7) Paper is coated to make finished paper.

8) Paper is cut into sheets and packaged.

Conserving Resources, pages 75–76

1. Sample answers:

I can reduce by...	I can reuse by...	I can recycle by...
- using paper on both sides - buying things that do not have a lot of packaging - bringing my own bags when shopping - drinking water from the tap instead of buying bottled water	- reusing wrapping paper and bags that gifts come in - donating things I do not want or selling them in a garage sale - making my own containers for pencils and other things from boxes or tins	- putting all paper, glass, and cans in recycling bins - composting food waste and using it for the garden - collecting rainwater to use on plants instead of tap water

2. If you use all the parts of an animal, you would end up with more useful items. You would also not have to use more resources to get all the things you made from that animal.

3. If you moved around during the year, you probably would not use all the resources in one place. Plant and animal resources would increase in number if you left them alone for a while.

4. Many people think humans are the most important things in the world and that their needs come above all other concerns.

Forms of Energy, pages 77–78

1. a) motion

b) motion

c) chemical

d) thermal

e) electrical

2. They are renewable because they are always available. They will never be used up.

3. They are non-renewable because they can be used up. They take millions of years to form.

4. Wind could be important in places where the wind blows all the time or most of the time. But wind could not be used in places where there is not a lot of wind.

5. Answers might include points such as the following: There are many types of fossil fuels in the world right now. Fossil fuels are often found in large areas. So when you dig a mine to get coal, there is a lot of coal to take out.

Word Stretch: Sample answer: *Biology* is the study of life. *Geography* is the study of land. A *hydroplane* is a type of boat that moves very fast over the surface of the water.

Fossil Fuels, pages 79–80

1. Sample answer: plants in swamps died → plants sank to the bottom of the swamp → plants formed peat → peat was covered by materials that turned into rock → more rock was formed → rock pressed down and squeezed the water out of the peat → peat turned into natural gas, oil, or coal

2. Sample answer: It would be easier to drill on land because the land does not move. You could put equipment on land and it would be safe. On the ocean, you would have to build something like a raft to put equipment on. The raft would move around, which would be dangerous. A drill in the ocean has to go all the way to the bottom before it hits ground.

3. Natural gas can be dangerous because it burns easily. If gas had no odour, you might not know when there was a gas leak. You might accidentally start a fire or cause an explosion. The added odour allows you to smell a gas leak and gives you a chance to leave the building. You could then call someone to fix the leak before a fire or explosion happens.

How We Use Energy, pages 81–82

1. Sample answers: Machines are used to make item and to perform tasks. All machines need energy to work. Many items such as cars and toys are made by machines in production plants. Machines are used to make natural resources into products such as copper and wood. Machines extract fossil fuels from the ground. They are also used to grow food on farms and to cut down forests. Because machines are used to do so many things, industries use a lot of energy.

2. People who use propane or wood might live away from towns and cities. They might not be able to get electricity or natural gas where they live. Some people might not want to use fossil fuels, so they would use wood instead.

3. Today, people have more appliances in their homes. People also have more electronic devices, such as televisions and CD players. Most homes have computers now, which was not the case 20 years ago.

4. Sample answer: The kitchen because of appliances that use energy.

How Does Energy Work? pages 83–84

1. Designs will vary. Ensure student designs follow the guidelines.

Energy Vocabulary, page 86

1. a) dump; It does not conserve resources.
b) biomass; It is a renewable energy source.
c) harvested; It is not a form of energy.
d) fossil fuels; It is a non-renewable energy source.

2. a) renewable
b) extracted
c) conservation
d) petroleum
e) transformation

3. Sample answer:
a) can be replaced by nature or through good management practices
b) pulled out, often with great force or effort
c) the preservation and protection of something; managing resources wisely
d) a dark oil brought up from under Earth's surface; a fossil fuel; also called crude oil
e) changing in form or shape

Conserving Energy, pages 87–89

1. Look for arguments supported by facts.
2. Natural gas, because it is a non-renewable resource so it will run out over time. Hydroelectricity is energy that comes from using water, and water is a renewable resource.
3. Sample answer: Solar power can only work where there is a lot of sunlight. Many places do not get enough sunlight. Solar power can only make energy during the day. We need energy all day and night. The energy made during the day may not be enough for the night, too.
4. Sample answers:
b) Turn out the lights when you leave a room.
c) Let your hair dry in the air instead.
d) Do not run the water all the time while brushing teeth.
e) Only wash clothes when you have a full load. Use cold water.
f) Take a shower instead of a bath.
g) Buy an energy-efficient television. Turn the television off when you leave the room.
h) Turn the computer off when you are not using it. Use a laptop instead of a desktop computer.
i) Do not use the heat cycle to dry the dishes. Open the dishwasher and let the dishes air dry.
j) Walk, ride a bike, or take a bus to school.

The Impact of Resource and Energy Use, pages 90–91

1. Sample answers:
a) support; There will be jobs building the dam and running the plant.
b) oppose; The dam would have negative affects on the plants and animals in the area.
c) support; The town needs money for things such as schools, hospitals, and building roads.
d) support; They may think local power costs less.
e) oppose; the number of fish would decrease and the fish might disappear

Take One Point of View, page 92

Answers will vary.

Satellites in Space, pages 101–103

1. Without satellites, people would not have satellite TV or GPS devices to give directions to a destination. (Some students might suggest that without weather information from satellites, weather forecasts would be less accurate.)
2. The satellite uses electricity stored in the rechargeable batteries.
3. The article says that the International Space Station is "our planet's most famous artificial satellite." The article also says that a satellite is "any object that circles, or orbits, a planet or another natural object in space." So the ISS must orbit Earth.